AF731103

PSYCHOLOGY OF ADJUSTMENT

PSYCHOLOGY OF ADJUSTMENT

(S.Y.B.A.)

(As Per Revised Syllabus w.e.f. 2009-2010)

Vipan B. Kumar

M.A., Ph.D., LLB.,

Reader and Head of the Department of Psychology,
R.D.National College, Bandra, Mumbai – 400 050
And
Summer Fellow, Albert Ellis Institute, New York, USA

First Edition: 2010

Himalaya Publishing House

MUMBAI • NEW DELHI • NAGPUR • BENGALURU • HYDERABAD • CHENNAI • PUNE • LUCKNOW • AHMEDABAD • ERNAKULAM • BHUBANESWAR • INDORE • KOLKATA

© AUTHOR

No part of this publication may be reproduced, stored in a retrieval system, or transmitted in any form or by any means, electronic, mechanical, photocopying, recording and/or otherwise without the prior written permission of the author and the publisher.

First Edition : 2010

Published by : Mrs. Meena Pandey
for **HIMALAYA PUBLISHING HOUSE PVT. LTD.,**
"Ramdoot", Dr. Bhalerao Marg, Girgaon, **Mumbai - 400 004.**
Phone: 2386 01 70/2386 38 63, Fax: 022-2387 71 78
Email: himpub@vsnl.com Website: www.himpub.com

Branch Offices:

New Delhi : "Pooja Apartments", 4-B, Murari Lal Street, Ansari Road, Darya Ganj, New Delhi - 110 002.
Phone: 23270392, 23278631, Fax: 011-23256286

Nagpur : Kundanlal Chandak Industrial Estate, Ghat Road, Nagpur - 440 018.
Phone: 011-2738731/3296733, Telefax: 0712-2721215

Bengaluru : No. 16/1 (Old 12/1), 1st Floor, Next to Hotel Highlands, Madhava Nagar, Race Course Road, Bengaluru - 560 001.
Phone : 080-22281541/22385461, Telefax: 080-22286611

Hyderabad : No. 3-4-184, Lingampally, Besides Raghavendra Swamy Matham, Kachiguda, Hyderabad - 500 027.
Phone: 040-27560041, 27550139, Mobile: 09848130433

Chennai : No. 85/50, Bazullah Road, T. Nagar, Chennai - 600 017.
Phone: 044-28144004/28144005

Pune : First Floor, "Laksha" Apartment, No. 527, Mehunpura, Shaniwarpeth, (Near Prabhat Theatre), Pune - 411 030. Phone: 020-24496323/24496333

Lucknow : Jai Baha Bhavan, Church Road, Near Manas Complex and Dr, Awasthi Clinic, Aliganj, Lucknow - 226 024
Phone: 0522-2339329, 4068914,
Mobile: 09305302158, 09415349385, 09389593752

Ahmedabad : 114, "SHAIL", 1st Floor, Opp. Madhu Sudan House, C.G. Road, Navrang Pura, Ahmedabad - 380 009.
Phone: 079-26560126, Mobile: 09327324149, 09314679413

Ernakulam : 39/104 A, Lakshmi Apartment, Karikkamuri Cross Rd., Ernakulam, Cochin - 622011, Kerala.
Phone: 0484-2378012, 2378016, Mobile: 09344199799

Bhubaneswar : 5 Station Square, Bhubaneswar - 751 001.
Mobile: 9861046007, E-mail: orissa@himpub.com

Indore : Kesardeep Avenue Extension, 73, Narayan Bagh, Flat No. 302, IIIrd Floor, Near Humpty Dumpty School, Narayan Bagh, Indore (M.P.) - 452 007. Mobile: 09301386468

Kolkata : 108/4, Beliaghata Main Road, Near ID Hospital, Opp. SBI Bank, Kolkata - 700 010. Mobile: 09910440956

DTP by : HPH, Editorial Office, Bhandup (Shubhangi)

Printed by : Sachin Printers, Mumbai.

PREFACE

Psychology of Adjustment is one of the most important subjects at the undergraduate level. This is one of the first books on this subject in India written by Indian Author and consists of topics which are not only of academic interest but would also engross the general reader interested in the subject.

The book contains 10 chapters in an easy to understand language with Indian examples. The book also contains guidelines for effective adjustment in day-to-day life. The topics discussed in the book range from self adjustment to adjustment in intimate relationships and sexuality. It also deals with adjustment with respect to various areas of our life including health, stress, friends, work and play. The book contains chapters dealing with understanding mental disorders, therapy, and treatment. It also contains a chapter which deals with grief and death.

Feedback as well as suggestions concerning the improvement of the book would be highly appreciated and acknowledged. The author can be contacted on his email: address: vipanbkumar@rediffmail.com for any further guidance and consultations.

Dr. Vipan B. Kumar

SYLLABUS

General Applied Component at S.Y.B.A. Option B - Psychology of Adjustment

Revised syllabus at the S.Y.B.A. to be brought into force with effect from the academic year 2009-2010

Objectives:-

1. To impart knowledge of the basic concepts and modern trends in Psychology of Adjustment
2. To foster interest in Psychology of Adjustment as a field of study and research
3. To make the students aware of the practical applications of the various concepts in Psychology of Adjustment in the Indian Context.
4. Lectures per week; 48 lectures per term; 9 lectures per topic and 3 lectures for discussion of Question paper pattern and the applications of important concepts in the syllabus.

Term 1 (Topics 1 to 5)

Topic 1. Self-direction in a Changing World and Seeking Self-hood

(a) Social Change
(b) The Challenge of Self-direction
(c) Themes of Personal Growth
(d) What is Self-concept; Core Characteristics of Self-concept
(e) The Self-concept and Personal Growth

Topic 2. Towards Better Health

(a) Body Image
(b) Psychological Factors and Physical Illness
(c) Coping with illness
(d) Promoting wellness

Topic 3. Taking Charge and Managing Motives and Emotions

(a) Mastery and Personal Control
(b) Personal Resolve and Decision Making; Decisions and Personal Growth

(c) Understanding Motivation
(d) Understanding Emotions

Topic 4. Making and Keeping Friends

(a) Meeting People
(b) Keeping Friends

Topic 5. At Work and Play

(a) Choosing Career
(b) Career Outlook
(c) Contemporary Issues in the World of Work
(d) Leisure Time

Term 2 (Topics 6 to 10)

Topic 6. Sexuality, Love and Commitment

(a) Men and Women; Sexual Responsiveness; Practical Issues
(b) Love and Intimacy; Commitment; Adjusting to Intimate Relationships
(c) Divorce and its Consequences

Topic 7. Stress

(a) Understanding Stress
(b) Reactions to Stress
(c) Managing Stress

Topic 8. Understanding Mental Disorders

(a) Psychological Disorders
(b) Anxiety Disorders
(c) Mood Disorders
(d) Other Common Disorders

Topic 9. Therapy and Treatment

(a) Insight Therapies
(b) Cognitive-Behavioural Therapies
(c) Other Approaches to Treatment
(d) How Well Does Therapy Work

Topic 10. Good Grief and Death

(a) Death and Dying
(b) Bereavement and Grief
(c) Life and Death in Perspective

CONTENTS

Social changes are occurring in very many areas of our life. Family life is getting influenced by such changes. More than 50% marriages are ending in divorce, increased live-in relationships, taking of important family functions such as food, clothing, child care, etc., by professional organizations have influenced human behavior and relationship to a great extent.

Developments in technology is influencing our life to a great extent. Communication, health, interpersonal relationships, work life, recreation are all influenced by technological developments. Some important effects of technology are as follows:

- Increased use of technology places greater demand on intellectual and technical knowledge.
- Work force composition is considerably changing. Educated middle class workers make up a larger proportion of the work force in comparison to blue-collar workers.
- Some individuals fear technology. Such a fear is called **technophobia.** These individuals are apprehensive about using computers as they fear that they will break the computers, make costly errors or look stupid.
- Research studies have revealed that individuals who are less educated, poor, and elderly or are disabled are less likely to use technology. In other words individuals who are less powerful, uses technology the least.
- Our society has moved from agricultural to industrial to service oriented sectors. There is a shift in orientation in a given economy as a result of introduction of technology. Changes in economic status has brought about far reaching social changes.
- One important type of change related to technology is increased pollution as well as anxiety related to health of our environment. Global warming, changes in environmental pollution is leading to wide variety of changes.
- Another significant change that has occurred with respect to social change is the increase in heterogeneity of the population. An increasing number of immigrants from various regions of the world are entering in many countries, especially U.S.A., U.K. and South Asian countries. With them they bring a wealth of cultural ideas languages, customs, etc. Increasing cultural diversity, due to globalization and telecommunication revolution has led to

social conflict and tensions as well as problems related to self identity.

THE CHALLENGE OF SELF-DIRECTION

Self-direction can be defined as the need to learn more about ourselves and our world as a means of directing our lives more effectively. The challenge of self-direction has raised many issues, some of which are briefly reviewed here:

- **Threat versus Challenge:** Many individuals respond to life events as threat. Others view it as a challenge. The perspective (viewpoint) that one adopts considerably influences one's approach. Some individuals may perceive the introduction of new technology at work place as a threat, others may view it as a challenge providing an individual with an opportunity to learn more about computers, technology, etc., and looking for opportunities to progress with new job openings.
- **Individualistic versus Collectivist Culture/Society:** Another relevant issue is whether you originally belong to individualistic or collectivist societies and at present you are working in which society. For Example: You might be born and reared in an individualistic society but today you are working in a collectivist society. This requires considerable adjustment and change in your personality and behavior. Inability to bring about adjustable changes can create conflict and maladjustment or reduce your work efficiency. Individualistic societies are those societies in which individual's gain is appreciated more than general societal gain. Collectivist societies are one in which collective or societal gain is cherished over individual advancement. In individualistic societies such as U.S.A., individuals enjoy personal freedom, independence from others and take greater pride in personal achievements than people in collectivist cultures. Individualistic societies also lead to considerable degree of insecurity, confusion and loneliness in an individual.
- **The Ambiguity of Personal Freedom:** Another issue related to self-direction is one's personal freedom and issues connected with it. Individuals in modern society have become obsessed and concerned with the issue of freedom and personal choice. A considerable degree of scholarly discussion on freedom has been done by Eric

Fromm. According to him human freedom has two fold meaning for people in the modern world:

- Freedom "from" traditional authorities such as state.
- Freedom "for" actualizing one's individual destiny.

Fromm holds that although people in advanced societies have been freed from the bonds of pre-individualistic society which gave them both security and limitations, they have not gained freedom in the positive sense of realizing their individual selves. Today, we have more freedom to direct our lives, especially, those related to daily life, crucial career and personal choices, etc. But the increased freedom, along with it has also brought anxiety, insecurity and isolation. According to Fromm, such isolation is so unbearable that many people are inclined to escape from the burden of freedom into new dependencies, such as: looking to experts for advise, government assistance, dependence on the crowd or social groups.

The ambiguity of human freedom becomes clearly evident when we make or see individuals making important decisions or choices about their lives. Some important examples that will reflect this ambiguity are as follows:

(i) Many individuals in the face of important decisions become anxious or "freeze-up".

(ii) Some individuals adopt a strategy of drifting. Instead of choosing how to live, people simple drift along, either by living according to the status quo or by dropping out or those whose lives are guided by no ties, code, tradition or major purpose.

(iii) Large majority of the individuals adopt a strategy of shared decision making, especially in areas such as community work, marriage, family life and assumed agreements among friends. Instead of really making a decision, people just talk until something happens. Very often individuals in intimate relationships presume a consensus, often never questioning it. If things go wrong no one feels responsible and blame each other or their luck.

(iv) Another commonly used strategy for making personal choice is that of appeal to some type of authority, which can be an expert, movement, religion or some institution. Individuals often take help of authority and go by norms established by such authority rather than their preferences or choices.

People who are autonomous do not rely on any of the above mentioned strategies. Such autonomous individuals are called self-actualized individuals. The concept of self-actualization was discovered by Abraham Maslow and other humanistic and existential scholars. Self-actualized individuals accept responsibility for their lives and carefully scrutinize the alternatives available to them. Self-actualized individuals also keep their eyes open and have the courage to admit when they are wrong and need to change. Many writers, artists, such as Alexander Solzhenitsyn, Arundhati Roy, etc., are examples of truly autonomous persons who made one decisive choice after another in order to maintain personal integrity and one's individuality. They often made these decisions against overwhelming criticism and danger in their oppressive societies.

Taking Charge of our Lives: Self-direction can be achieved when we learn to take charge of our lives. Taking charge of our lives means that we can and must choose for ourselves. Many younger individuals, today have more freedom than what their parents had when they were young. Too much freedom has also added many constraints and anxieties.

(a) According to Fromm, increased freedom has also brought along with it the necessity to take decision. We are required to take many decisions due to increased freedom. This creates anxiety and stress.

(b) Taking a decision in the background of freedom is not an easy task. Individuals feel anxious about and experience fear of making the wrong decisions.

(c) Increased freedom has created many uncertainties.

Our decisions are highly dynamic and change as we mature and grow. Our decisions are never perfect; at a given time there are many constraints which influence our decisions - such as time, availability of limited resources, lack of knowledge, etc.

Taking charge of our lives also means that we should assume responsibility for our choices, without blaming others or our fate. Individuals who have charge of their lives are internally motivated and self actualized. These people experience less interpersonal distress and more interpersonal closeness with others. Such individuals also indulge in altruism, which is the desire or ability to help others, even at cost to the helper. Taking charge of our lives also means indulging in altruistic behavior. Taking charge of our lives involves three things:

- Freedom to make choice.
- Assuming responsibility.
- Indulging in prosocial behavior.

Taking charge of our lives is not an easy task:

- It leads to considerable degree of stress and hardships.
- It also gives rise to many negative emotions and feelings such as anger, resentment, frustration, anxiety, etc.
- When we take charge of our lives we become prone to hurt and disappointment. There are also higher chances of interpersonal conflict.
- Taking charge of our lives requires courage. Paul Tillich calls it as the "courage to be", i.e., the courage to affirm ourselves and our possibilities in spite of the risks involved.

When we fail to take charge of our lives we also fail to adapt to situations as well as we fail to grow. This leads to difficulties in adjustment and influences our personality. One can learn to take charge by developing new skills, learning new things and bringing changes in one's life.

Challenge of Living in Today's Individualistic Society: Living in today's individualistic society is a challenging phenomenon. It exposes us to many threats and dangers. We have to be highly cautious and aware of not only ourselves but also of the environment around us. Accidents, terrorist attacks, victimization, exposure to AIDS, infection and medical illness, etc., are potential dangers around us, which we should guard ourselves against. Individuals in today's materialistic society have become highly impatient and are motivated to seek immediate and direct gratification.

Individuals in today's individualistic society have become more concerned with their personal rights rather than their social responsibilities. This obsession with their life's self-direction is making them relentlessly pursue their own interests and goals, at the risk of violating the rights of others. They are also less likely to be co-operating or compromising and less likely to accommodate others views or preferences. One Example of obstinately pursuing one's own needs at the expense of others is Road Rage.

THEMES OF PERSONAL GROWTH

Personal growth is a time consuming process requiring constant adjustments, learning and changing our strategy. Personal growth manifests itself when we react to our environment; learn to deal with contradictions and uncertainties surrounding our lives. The following are some important themes related to personal growth:

1. Living with contradictions and uncertainty.
2. Continuity and change.
3. The experience of personal growth.
4. Beyond individualism.

We would discuss each of them in brief:

1. Living with Contradiction and Uncertainty: The life of a modern technological man, to a large extent, is filled with contradiction and uncertainty, which to a great extent influences personal growth. We constantly experience conflict and have to learn to resolve conflicting values, rules and actions.

The task of reconciling between old and new values is very difficult for a middle class, educated individual who is well informed. Our tradition on the one hand and scientific development on the other hand is creating increased conflict and contradictory situation. Individuals who are less educated and cultured are more confused and upset while dealing with contradictions surrounding them.

Personal and social change which gives rise to contradiction is not easy to resolve or handle. In many cases these personal or social changes generate grossly unrealistic expectations leading to disappointment.

There is increased uncertainty in our life. Bomb blast in a train, terrorist attack, highjacking a plane, robbery or mob attack in a train, etc., can occur suddenly and without any warning, disrupting our life and health.

Personal growth involves learning to deal with various contradictions and uncertainties of life. Modern psychology and scientific development can provide dependable information about us and our world, but the mastery and effective use of this knowledge is up to an individual.

2. Continuity and Change: One of the important issues related to personal growth is concerning change and stability among individuals. Do individuals change in the process of growing up? Can our personalities really change, or do they remain stable over life time. Why do individuals change and why some people resist change. Early in the history of psychology "Nature versus Nurture" debate was very common. Those who believed in nature were of the opinion that genes and early experiences were important influences that shaped our development. In contrast those who believed in environmental influences (The nurture view) were of the opinion that environmental forces, i.e., socio cultural factors considerably shape our development. Both nature as well as nurture plays an important role in influencing our adjustment and personal growth. However, psychologists disagree among themselves as to what is more important, Nature or Nurture. Research studies have revealed that people continue to grow and develop throughout their lives. Both continuity and change influence our personal growth.

Robert McCrae and Paul Costa (1994) found that there is stability of personality throughout the lifespan. The highest degree of stability was in the area of "introversion- extroversion", which reflects gregariousness, warmth and assertiveness. Individuals were also found to be stable with respect to "neuroticism" which includes traits such as depression and hostility.

Longitudinal studies (studies in which same individual is followed over a long period of time) have revealed that there are changes in an individual's personality due to personal maturity and life experiences. Some research studies have revealed that as people grow their stability becomes more evident.

Research studies have also demonstrated that certain aspects of personality, especially social and emotional style such as introversion-extroversion, anxiety and depression remain stable over a period of time. Changes in following personality characteristics occur over a period of time.

- Self esteem
- Sense of personal mastery
- Control over their environment
- Values

Some other important findings with respect to stability and change are as follows:

- How much personal growth and change in a desirable direction we want depends on the different priorities we assign to stability or change.
- People with traditional values tend to exhibit a high degree of stability in their lives unless something happens to make them change.
- Deeply ingrained patterns of behavior can be changed only when something dramatic happens such as unwanted divorce, death of a child, failure in one's career or being a victim of a terrorist attack.
- Those who value personal growth, choice and personal freedom may continue changing to a greater extent throughout their lives.
- To believe we can change is one thing; to pursue and actively achieve personal change is something else.
- Experience of change can be confusing, stressful and unsettling for many individuals, especially when they are not prepared or oriented to change in their lives.

3. The Experience of Personal Growth: Personal growth is a unique experience. Our inner experience of growth tends to be uneven, with spurts and plateaus.The experience of personal growth follows a three phase cycle

- Acknowledging change
- A sense of dissonance and dissatisfaction
- Reorganizing our experience

Acknowledging Change: Growth usually begins with acknowledgement of change. Change occurs all the time. Sometimes it is evident, at most times it is subtle and gradual. We are not always aware about change, For example: we are not always aware about the change in our height or weight, but someone who sees us after a long time would be able to clearly notice it and make a comment with respect to it. We become more accurately aware of changes at some moments than at others. Sometimes we become aware of change rather suddenly, For example: by receiving unexpected criticism or compliments. We also change to a great extent under the following conditions:

- When uncertain or unexpected events occur.
- While indulging in decision making, such as which career or college to choose.

- Taking up new responsibilities such as marriage, parenthood, promotion, etc.
- Disappointments and failures such as being fired from a job without warning also forces us to acknowledge change.

A Sense of Dissonance or Dissatisfaction: A sense of dissonance and dissatisfaction leads us towards change. If we react to a given situation defensively, with little awareness of our real feelings, we may fail to adapt and grow and may not change. In contrast, when someone feels disappointment, he/she may be actually aroused or motivated to seek further change. Growth cycle can be triggered by disappointment and failure as well as by success.

It should also be remembered that when our motive for growth proceeds out of a sense of challenge or mastery, we may be more stimulated and less apprehensive about the outcome and may work towards change. Experiencing dissatisfaction in a relationship, work or any situation can make us indulge in change. Sometimes, people who are bored with their routine life seek change and indulge in strange activities such as deviant or non-conventional sexual activity, drug experience, etc., leading to increased probability of developing HIV/AIDS or encounter with law.

Reorganizing our Experience: It means acquiring new ideas and then in response alter our attitudes, behavior and values. Becoming aware of our unconscious process by participating in group activity, undergoing a counseling session, etc., can help an individual to make changes in his/her behavior attitudes. At times we may listen to advice or opinions of others, i.e., our parents, teachers, sports instructors or some other expert and bring changes in our-self because we know that the person wants to help rather than hurt us.

Growth may also take the form of new self perceptions, such as increased self acceptance and confidence that comes with an achievement such as earning a professional degree. It should be remembered that each inner adjustment or change we make affects the whole or our experience, so that growth consists of the continuous reorganization of that experience.

4. Beyond Individualism: America, urban India as well as most democratic societies are becoming highly individualistic. Increased individualism often limits our growth. Many Americans today act independent of any cultural or social influence, being responsible to the self alone. As a result, increased individualism is making us become less committed to societal and community goals. A few decades ago an urban Indian was held in check by strong ties to family, church, religion and community. But now these ties are weakening, people are putting aside the public concerns that are necessary for the survival of a free and caring society.

During crisis that affects a nation or community as a whole, people keep aside their petty differences, racial hatreds and attitudinal conflicts. They act more as members of community, even to the extent of sacrificing some of their individual interest for liberty.

Self-fulfillment does not necessarily require individuals to withdraw from the social involvement necessary for democratic living. Self–fulfillment can be enhanced if one becomes socially integrated and meaningfully involves in community life.

WHAT IS SELF-CONCEPT: CORE CHARACTERISTICS OF SELF-CONCEPT

Self-concept is the overall image or awareness we have of our self. It includes all those perspectives of "I" and "Me" together with feelings, beliefs and values associated with them. Self-concept is actually a complex concept made "of" a multiplicity of selves even though we refer to it in the singular.

We often take our Self-concept for granted, as when we are engaged in an activity at work or play. At other times we are very much aware of ourselves, as when we are making an important decision, taking on a heavy responsibility or feeling embarrassed. Individuals often become self conscious when they experience a discrepancy between their self image and the way they appear to others. Our self-concept exerts a powerful influence, affecting the way we perceive, indulge and behave.

The Self-concept provides us, as well as others, with a personal identity or sense of who we are. Our Self-concept gives coherence and consistency to our thoughts and actions. We often incorporate information about ourselves into our Self-concept. We actually manage our Self-concept so as to maintain a positive view of ourself. We generally seek positive information about ourselves from our friends and families and from our performance at work or in school or elsewhere. According to Psychologists individuals adopt a self-serving attribution bias. Attribution is the process of attributing or ascribing the cause of some event. We make internal attribution to the self or external attribution to the environment. With regards to our self we commonly choose self-serving attribution. Self-serving attribution are those that glorify the self or conceive the self as causing the good outcomes that come our way. For example, we often take personal credit for our success but blame external causes for our failures.

Types of Self-concept: Within our Self-concept we have many different types of self. The four most important types of Self-concept are as follows:

1. Body Image: The awareness about our bodies.
2. Self Image: The image I see myself to be.
3. The Ideal Self: The self I would like to be.
4. The Social Self: The ways I feel others see me.

We would discuss some important types of self. The topic of Body Image is covered in detail in the next chapter.

1. Self Image: Self image is the way we see our self. It is the self you think you are. It is made up of highly personal images. Our Self image is highly private. Each one of us is an expert and knows about one's self image. Our Self image is made up of the many self perceptions we have acquired in the process of growing up, especially in our formative years or early years.

Our Self image is mostly influenced by the way we are seen and treated by significant others, especially by our parents or romantic partners. When we are young and impressible, we tend to internalize what they thought of us (their judgement about us, expectations from us and their evaluations about us) and regarded ourselves accordingly.

Our Self images are revised depending upon the experiences we have with others, especially with our friends, lovers, teachers and spouses. A great deal of change in a self image comes from adapting to different people and situation.

2. Ideal Self: It is the self you would like to be, including your aspiration, moral ideals and values. According to psychoanalytic view, individuals are not fully aware of their ideal self. According to them many of our "shoulds" and "should nots" of our conscience represents unconscious and unrealistic demands that may keep us from growing. If our ideal self is very much different from how others see us, the result is social anxiety or extreme shyness that can interfere with our daily life.

Our Ideal Self serves as an incentive for us to do our best. When we fail to live up to our ideal self there are two things we can do:

- Redouble our effort to achieve our aspirations.
- Modify them (i.e., our desires, aspiration, etc.) in the direction of more fruitful goals.

3. Multiple Selves: It is also called as Self Complexity. We do not have one self. Our sense of self is a collection of many different selves that each one of us possesses. Self complexity can be defined as the extent to which one's self-concept is comprised of many differentiated self aspects; which can include hundreds of different types of self perceptions. Our self-concept can include the following:

- Gender Role
- Body Image
- Racial Identity
- Work or Occupational Identity, etc.

There are individual differences with respect to self complexity, with some individuals having more complicated self concepts as compared to others. Multiple aspects of self can also vary greatly from culture to culture. For examples, the self construct of Japanese often include familial self as well as spiritual self neither of which plays a prominent part in the self constructs of white Americans.

Our various selves, generally exhibits certain consistency or organizing pattern as a whole. We refer to them collectively as the self-concept. People with fragmented, incoherent view of themselves – such as the severely emotionally disordered – are often unsure of who they are and may behave in a highly inconsistent manner. In contrast, those who have achieved a more desirable integration of our various selves may feel a clever sense of personal identity and behave in a somewhat more consistent manner.

Core Characteristics of Self-Concept: Our self-concept is helpful, dynamic and not rigid. Our self-concept is not like a strait-jacket that once acquired, during our formative years, cannot be further changed. Our self-concept is like a loosely fitting garment that is continuously being altered with experience.

Once established, the core of the self-concept generally exhibits a high degree of stability. Peripheral aspects of the self can, and often do, change rather quickly.

Our self-concept serves as a filter through which we view our experiences, so that experiences that are not consistent with self-concept are apt to be distorted and kept out of awareness.

Under core characteristics of self-concept we would discuss the following topics:

1. Self-consistency
2. Self-esteem
3. Self-enhancement and Self-verification

1. Self-Consistency: It refers to a tendency to perceive our experiences in a manner consistent with our self-concept. Significant others (i.e., those people who are significant to us in our life such as our parents, brother, sister, etc.) have a great effect on our self-concept and self-consistency.

According to Carl Rogers experiences that are consistent with our self-concept tend to be perceived accurately and admitted fully into our conscious awareness. These self perceptions make up the core of our self-concept. Experiences that are not consistent with both our sensory experiences and our self-concept are perceived more selectively and sometimes inaccurately, such experiences are either distorted or kept away from awareness.

Experiences that are not consistent with our learned self-concept might be perceived as too threatening and consequently may not be accurately perceived or labeled and may be kept away from awareness either in part or whole.

We often use defense mechanism to boost our self-concept and achieve self-consistency. Two important defense mechanism that we often use to enhance our self-concept are as follows:

- Self Immunization
- Mnenomic Neglect

Self Immunization: It involves trivializing threatening information, such as failure, by making the behaviors seems less important.

Mnenomic Neglect: It refers to poor recall (or forgetting) of negative feedback that is inconsistent with core aspects of the self-concept.

2. Self-esteem: It is one of the most important aspects of our self-concept. It can be defined as the personal evaluation of ourselves and the resulting feelings of worth associated with our self-concept.Our self-esteem is influenced by wide variety of factors, some of which include the following:

- Childhood experiences.
- Our own standards or Ideal Self.
- Our general culture.
- Family factors, etc.
- Success or failure.
- Social comparison and reference groups also influence our self esteem.

It has been observed that individuals with high Self-esteem had parents:-

- Who were highly supportive.
- Expressed a lot of affection.
- Established firm but reasonable rules.

It has also been observed that individuals with low self esteem usually were brought up by parents who relied on parenting style that were overly strict, overly permissive or inconsistent. Our self esteem is also influenced by success and failure. Psychologists, once thought, that a backlog of stored success enhanced self-esteem and repeated failure undermined it.

One's self esteem is also influenced by how we explore our self to reference groups and our fear of social rejection by our group. The process of using others to compare ourselves to in order to understand who we are relative to them is known as social comparison. Thus, individuals with similar talents and success may vary in their self-esteem, depending on whom they compare themselves with.

Types of Self-esteem: There are two types of self-esteem:

- Global Self-Esteem
- Specific Self-Esteem

High self-esteem is both beneficial as well as a curse. High self-esteem correlates better with:

(i) Academic performance.

(ii) Job performance.

(iii) Better interpersonal relationship.

High self-esteem is also a blessing because people with high self-esteem perform better in groups and are likelier to persist in the face of failure than people with low self-esteem. It has been observed that both high and low self-esteem is associated with relationship breakups:

- People with high self-esteem often exit from bad relationship, hence they breakup.
- People with low self-esteem often find themselves in an unhappy relationship.
- High self-esteem has few negative sides besides relationship breakups.
- High self-esteem is related to antisocial behaviors such as cheating on tests and annoying or interrupting others. For examples bullies have overly inflated self-esteem.
- High self-esteem has been found to be correlated with cigarette smoking, alcohol and drug abuse, premarital sex, etc.

3. Self-enhancement and Self-verification: Self-enhancement Theory states that people will try to get positive feedback that affirms their own ideas about their positive qualities. Most people prefer and seek out positive feedback about themselves, but mostly for those attribute that they themselves view as positive, primarily because positive self views are generally adaptive. Self-verification Theory states that people want to preserve their own images (both positive and negative) of themselves and therefore elicit feedback that verifies or confirms their own self-perceptions. Self-verification gives us a sense of stability or consistency in an unpredictable world. Also such confirmation is vital to social interaction because if others see us as we see ourselves, they will have a better idea of how to treat us, what to expect of us, etc.

Self-concept and Personal Growth: Our Self-concept continues to change as we mature and develop. For example, it has been noted by some researchers that self-esteem is relatively high in childhood, drops during adolescence (particularly for girls), rises gradually throughout adulthood and then declines in old age. With respect to Self-concept and personal growth following topics are worth discussing:

1. The self you would like to be (i.e. visualization or guided imagery)
2. Social selves
3. Learning from criticism
4. Greater self-direction

We would discuss each of these briefly:

1. The self you would like to be (i.e., visualization or guided imagery): It is one promising approach to self improvement and personal growth. Visualization (or guided imagery) is a procedure that helps a person shut off the outside world and bypass the censor we call the brain, enabling the person to see, experience and learn from an intuitive feeling, unconscious nature.

Visualizing our "possible selves", including the desired as well as feared selves, helps you not only to attain goals but to cope more effectively with the present.Visualization has many practical benefits:-

- It has been successfully used in health psychology to enhance the comfort of people undergoing chemotherapy to treat cancer.
- Visualizing our possible selves may help to cope with present life difficulties.
- Visualizing helps you to change yourself. Rigid mental images of our possible selves may help us to become the person we would like to be, especially when accompanied by the appropriate efforts.

2. Social selves: The term Social selves refer to the impression we think others have of us. It is the way we think they view us, which may not be an accurate representation of their actual views. We have many different social selves as there are distinct groups of persons about whose opinions we care. We see ourselves differently with each person we meet.

(a) With stranger, we may be guarded and unsure of ourselves, at least until we get to know what kind of person we are dealing with.

(b) A bossy, critical employer may make us feel anxious and inferior.

(c) Close friend who admires and compliments us, makes us feel confident and affectionate.

We often make errors in assessing feedback that we receive from others. One such type of errors is called as "spotlight effect", in which we overestimate how salient our behavior, appearance and emotions are to others.

It has also been observed (Gilorich and Savitsky (1999)) that because our own self-incrimination are so harsh; most individuals expect others to judge them more harshly than they really do.

The way we see ourselves is also virtually affected by the way we behave in different roles and situations. For example, in office we may be a leader but on the homefront we may be subjugated and docile.

Our self image is greatly changed by many factors around us such as:

- Routinization
- The complexity of tastes
- Advancement
- Fringe benefits
- Peers, etc.

Our self is considered affected by sound and cultural influences. It is due to such influences that we give importance to social roles and social relationships.

3. Learning from criticism: We do not like to hear criticism about ourselves, even when we are wrong. This is largely due to reason that people feel that criticism is a personal attack that they must defend themselves against all costs. An average individual wastes a lot of time and energy worrying about criticism, justifying themselves and going to great lengths to avoid it. Accepting criticism can become a valuable means of personal growth. Some people are more open to criticism and they believe in the following statements:

- "Criticism tells me where the other person is coming from, how that person sees me and what he/she expects of me".
- Your critics can tell you where you are going wrong before your friends can.
- Criticism can often serve as a valuable source of new information to be evaluated objectively.

Some important points with respect to criticism are as follows:

(i) If several people offer the same criticism for the same behavior, there's a good chance that the criticism is valid and should be acted on.

(ii) People often feel they are being criticized unfairly, especially, when they are under stress.

(iii) Even criticism spoken in frustration or anger needs your attention.

(iv) Getting emotionally aroused as a result of criticism is generally not good for your work performance. Emotional arousal tends to interfere with your ability to perform as well as lowering your self confidence.

(v) You should take positive steps to put the required changes into action, so that we don't waste energy defending ourself.

4. Greater Self-Direction: Individuals achieve personal growth when they move towards greater self-direction. Humanistic writers such as Carl Rogers and Abraham Maslow have done considerable research with respect to self-direction. Greater self-direction involves the process of becoming. Rogers found that in the process of becoming individual's growth follows a general pattern.

(a) According to Rogers, we revise ourself as we grow up, self revision involves a movement in which you move away from certain values, attitudes, ideas, etc., which you have internalized from your parents. You also change the various distorted self perceptions which you have acquired in the process of growing up.

(b) As individuals grow and develop they sort out aspects of the self that they have acquired under social pressure or as a result of the desire to be accepted. Some self-perceptions are affirmed and strengthened, others are modified or rejected. It is due to this reasons that some adolescents show negativism or young adult leave their home.

As individuals grow and reach a stage of self-actualization they achieve greater self-direction and self-acceptance, Individuals become more open and trusting of their own experiences. Individuals also become more accepting of others as they come to accept themselves. When you begin to accept others you attempt to over come self-alienation. In short, personal growth involves:

(i) Moving away from some of the familiar self-images acquired during the formative years.

(ii) Seeing yourself in new ways, especially as a more self directed person.

(iii) Understanding the general pattern of growth.

(iv) Using feedback from others in positive manner so as to achieve greater self awareness.

(v) Personal growth involves learning to trust oneself and being open to oneself.

Questions

1. Write short notes on the following:
   (a) Principles of Self-direction
   (b) Social Change
   (c) Challenge of Self-direction.
2. Discuss the themes of Personal Growth.
3. Define Self-concept and discuss its core characteristics.
4. Write short notes on the following:
   (a) Types of Self-esteem
   (b) Self-concept and Personal Growth.

****

2 Towards Better Health

BODY IMAGE

Many of us are very much familiar with our body. We spend considerable time bathing, touching or grooming ourselves. We also acquire considerable information about our bodies through feedback from others. When others tell us how we look or make comments about our physical features, etc. Our body image is an approximate perception of what we really are. Our bodies are constantly changing and some aspects of this changing body image may not be perceived by us such as the ageing man who had difficulty in recognizing the wrinkles on his face, his thinning hair or his sagging waistline.

Our awareness of the insides of our bodies is even less well formed. Many of us may not be aware of:

- Our innate needs/drives.
- The significance of various aches and pains.
- Interpret approximately the various bodily states, etc.

Some individuals are not intimately attached to their bodies. Such a condition is called as depersonalization or unembodiment. It can be defined as the sense of not being intimately attached to one's body. Depersonalisation is generally experienced by individuals who suffer from certain types of psychiatric illness or one who has taken hallucinogenic drugs. Individuals who take hallucinogenic drugs may feel that parts of their bodies usually their hands do not belong to them.

Definition of Body Image: Body image refers to the mental image we form of our own bodies. Body image is one aspect of our self-concept. In recent years the concept of body image has been expanded to include how we feel about our bodies as well as how satisfied or dissatisfied we are with our bodies. A study by David Garner (1997) published in Psychology Today, has noted the following:

- Many people are dissatisfied with their bodies.
- Women, in general, were less satisfied as compared to men with their appearance.
- Overall more people are dissatisfied with their bodies than ever before.

The rate at which we are dissatisfied with our bodies is rapidly accelerating across time. Most individuals cited their weight and dissatisfaction with their abdominal areas in particular as the reason for their dissatisfaction.

A recent study carried out in USA by the Center for Disease Control and Prevention (2001) found that female students are more likely to believe that they are overweight as compared to male students. Women are more concerned about body image and weight control than men because of the influences of mass media and greater emphasis on physical appearance for women than for men. Entertainment celebrities (such as film stars), fashion models and well known sports personalities were identified by many men and women as having influenced their body image.Teasing by others and parental attitudes also influence one's body image.

Ideal Body: Related to body image is the concept of ideal body; which can be defined as the body we would like to have. The body ideal is our image of the ideal body. Our ideal body is greatly influenced by the particular body ideals prevalent in our culture. For e.g., In Jamaican society plumpness is desirable. Hence, the desire for plumpness is strong enough to counteract foreign preoccupation with thinness.

Media and one's culture considerably determines as to what is an ideal body. The ideal man is tall, large, muscular and energetic. The ideal woman is slim, shapely, smooth-skinned, young, glamorous and often blonde. The media defines beauty so narrowly that few of us only feel satisfied. Individuals who don't fit media images tend to have negative feelings about themselves. making it difficult for them to accept themselves as they are.

There are individual differences as well as sex differences with respect to ideal body. Individuals of both sexes hold body ideals that are somewhat different from their actual bodies. The average man wants to be an inch or so taller than he is and have broader shoulders and a more muscular build. The average woman wants to be an inch or so taller and somewhat thinner than she is.

Men and Women differ with respect to their perception of what they think that the opposite sex would prefer. For e.g., college aged women think men want a women who is even thinner with larger breasts then women themselves want. There is less discrepancy between men's perception of the ideal male body.

The concern with appearance lessens with age.Young adolescents are more concerned with their appearance. One's physical features continue to be a subject of great concern for people of all ages.

PSYCHOLOGICAL FACTORS AND PHYSICAL ILLNESS

There is an intimate connection between Psychological factors and causation of physical illness. The relationship between psychological factors and physical illness is very old and was expressed as mind-body problem. Even Greek physicians observed that mind, to a great extent, influences the development of many physical illnesses.

Medical science has discovered that there is a two way relationship between mind and body. The term 'Mind' includes psychological factors, emotional factors, etc. The term body is used to refer to physical influences such as organic factors (genes, brain, and neurotransmitters), physical states and conditions, etc. There is considerable evidence which shows that organic factors contribute to the major psychological disorders such as Schizophrenia, major depression and manic depression (bipolar disorder). A large number of research studies have also revealed that psychological factors influence our susceptibility and resistance to physical illness. It is now held that psychological factors can affect any physical condition not just so called psychosomatic illness.

Recent research has pointed out that psychologists today adopt systems perspective which held the view that biological, psychological and social systems interact to influence physical illness. It has been noted by almost all Psychologists that negative emotions and stress makes an individual susceptible to physical illness.

In this section, we would discuss four important psychological factors that influence physical illness. These are as follows:

1. The Immune System
2. Personality
3. Lifestyle Choices
4. Environmental Issues

We would discuss the contribution of each in influencing physical illness.

1.The Immune System: It can be defined as a complex surveillance system including the brain and various blood cells that defend our bodies by identifying and destroying various foreign invaders. Our immune system makes us vulnerable to certain illness. Immune system can be inherently weak or it can become weak as a result of increased stress. Psychological research has revealed two important facts related to stress and immune system.

(a) Psychological processes such as depression prevents us from taking positive health related measures, such as eating well, regular exercises, etc., thereby weakening our immune system.

(b) In stressful situations, body's immune system functions less well. Stress lowers the body's resistance and a variety of physical ailments ranging from herpes to upper respiratory infections.

2. Personality: Certain personality traits help us to resist diseases, on the other hand certain personality traits can lead to development of certain illness. Personality traits influence our attitudes, beliefs, values and corresponding behavior. Five important personality traits that have received increasing research attention are as follows:

(a) openness to experience (being open minded about novelty).
(b) conscientiousness (diligence).
(c) agreeableness (being good natured).
(d) extroversion (being friendly).
(e) emotional stability (anxious and somewhat irrational).

Goodwin and Engstron (2002) found that good health was correlated with following personality traits:

- Openness to experience.

- Extroversion.
- Conscientiousness.

Poor health was found to be correlated with emotional instability.

One important personality factor that pertains to our ability to resist illness is self-efficacy, which can be defined as the belief in one's capabilities to organize and execute actions required to produce given attainments. Self-efficacy helps us to adopt healthy and preventive behaviours. Individuals high in self-efficacy are more likely to adapt healthy lifestyles. They are also able to adhere to their regimens when they decide to overcome certain unhealthy behaviors. High self-efficacy can be developed in following ways:

- Individuals must learn to monitor their own behaviour, especially the ones which they wish to change.
- They must set short-range attainable goals to motivate and direct their own efforts.
- Enlist positive social support from others to help them sustain the efforts needed to succeed.

3. Lifestyle Choices: Our lifestyle choices are another important psychological factor that may play an important role in development of certain physical illnesses. For e.g., Development of certain habits, one's choice of a given work or field of study. The choice to life in a particular environment considerably influences our health and development of physical illness. Three important hazards that are directly associated with lifestyle and that can be controlled are as follows:

(a) Obesity

(b) Tobacco Abuse and Smoking

(c) Alcohol and Drug Abuse

We would discuss each of these briefly

(a) Obesity: It can be defined as an excessive amount of body fat, usually defined as exceeding the desirable weight for one's height, build and age by 20 percent or more. Obesity is associated with an increased risk of illness and death from diabetes, high blood pressure, strokes, coronary heart disease, kidney and gall bladder disorders, high cholesterol and some forms of cancers.

- It has been estimated that obese individuals have a 50 to 100 per cent increased risk of death from all causes compared with normal-weight individuals.

- Very obese people suffer more surgical and anesthetic complications than leaner people.
- Child birth among obese women may be more risky for both mother and child.

Obesity is a growing problem in modern technological society. The prevalence of obesity varies in different cultural groups. There are no sex differences in obesity. Though the psychological perception of being overweight varies. It is more common among women. In other words, women are more disturbed by overweight than men. Obesity is a major health hazard as it is associated with the following illnesses.

- High blood pressure
- Diabetes
- Heart disease, etc.

Obesity also has a social stigma attached to it and many individuals hold the belief that obese individuals are unhealthy, lazy, and selfish. Obesity is a multi causational and complex problem involving the following areas:

- Genetic factors
- Metabolic problems
- Nutritional factors
- Psychological factors
- Socio cultural factors
- Medical factors

(b) Tobacco Abuse and Smoking: Tobacco is a major health hazard. Tobacco abuse can be defined as the abuse of tobacco to such an extent that heart, respiratory and other health related problems develop. Cigarette smoking is a major factor in heart disease, lung cancer, emphysema and other fatal illness. Smoking also contributes to many forms of cancer: mouth, larynx, bladder and pancreas.

Smokers who also drink alcohol magnify their risks of cancer even more because it enhances the carcinogenic effect of tobacco at certain sites of the body such as esophagus, mouth and larynx.

Smoking is a difficult habit to break. It has been found that half or more of those who quit smoking eventually resume the habit. In addition to the psychological dependence on the smoking habit, nicotine which is there in cigarette, is considered to be physically addictive. Smokers often build tolerance to nicotine and need to smoke a large number of cigarettes or ones with higher nicotine content to get the same effect. Withdrawal from habitual smoking or nicotine produces variety of symptoms;

- Nervousness
- Headaches and dizziness
- Fatigue
- Sweating
- Insomnia
- Cramps, tremors and
- Heart palpitations

Approaches to overcome Smoking or Nicotine Addiction: Some important approaches to overcome nicotine addiction are as follows:

(i) Patch: In recent years many people have begun using the "patch" which, when attached to one's arm, releases nicotine into body, thereby reducing the physical craving for a smoke.

(ii) Stimulus Control: One approach for overcoming habit of smoking is stimulus control. In this approach, smokers are made aware of the stimuli and the situations that trigger their smoking.

(iii) Social Support: Smokers increase their chances of success through the support of friends, spouses or support groups.

(c) Alcohol and Drug Abuse: It is another health hazard related to lifestyle choices. Alcohol and Drug Abuse refer to the misuse or dependence on a psychoactive substance like alcohol or drugs. Alcohol use constitutes a major health hazard. Nearly 2/3rd of the drivers in fatal accidents have been drinking alcohol. Automobile accidents involving alcohol are a leading cause of death among youths. Chronic heavy drinking is often accompanied by poor nutrition and results in serious damage to many parts of the body such as liver, etc. Drug abuse is another major health hazard:

- Overdose from barbiturates is a common means of committing suicide.
- People who attempt to stop smoking barbiturates or sleeping pills often experience a rebound effect that disturbs their sleep.

- Excessive and prolonged use of tranquilizers especially among the elderly may damage the respiratory system, kidneys and liver.

Some important dangers of taking drugs are as follows:

- Combining alcohol with drugs tend to multiply the effect of the drug.
- Use of illegal or street drug poses special problems. There is no control over the strength or purity of the drug. Individuals may often damage their bodies or take a fatal overdose by mistake.

Treatment of alcohol and drug abuse is not an easy task. Though wide variety of programs are available for treating drug abuse, some have a relatively high failure rate. Individuals may not be ready for the complete change in lifestyle demanded by the program. Relapse rate in alcohol and drug treatment is high.

(d) Environmental Issues: The environment, physical as well as socio-cultural, in which we find ourselves, more or less, contributes towards wide variety of health problems. Air, water and noise pollution, over crowding, etc., can create health problems. It has also been demonstrated that social and psychological environment can at times be toxic.

Exposure to mass media, television, songs which encourage illicit drug use, unprotected sex, etc., can be a major cause of subsequent health problems.

Another feature of environment that is not conducive to wellness is when the factors in the environment are ambiguous. Ambiguity often creates distress. Many individuals cannot cope with a situation/environment that is uncontrollable, unpredictable, ambiguous and unresolvable.

COPING WITH ILLNESS

Coping with illness is a skillful task that requires good decision making skills and taking certain actions. One can cope with illness in a much better manner if he/she does the following:

1. Noticing and Interpreting Symptoms.
2. Seeking Help.
3. Adhering to Treatment.

We would discuss each of these in brief

1. Noticing and Interpreting Symptoms: Many illnesses can be predicted in its initial stages if we are well versed with its symptoms. Ignoring the initial symptoms or body reactions can create serious complications once the illness has developed to its full blown form. Learning the warning signs of certain illness as cancer, cardiac problems, viral fever, etc., can help us to take quick steps and avoid subsequent complications.

Individuals differ how they react and interpret their body symptoms. Some individuals are highly sensitive. They habitually complain of unfounded ailments or exhibit an undue fear of illness, such individuals are called as hypochondriacs. On the other hand, some individuals often ignore, down play or under report their symptoms. Such individuals are called as Extroverts. These individuals are warm, outgoing and maybe sufficiently involved in life so that they don't have time to complain or notice their ailments. Individuals high in hypochondriasis report 2 or 3 times as many symptoms as better adjusted persons. On the other hand, those high in extroversion generally report fewer ailments.

Coping Strategies: Some important coping strategies related to health concerns are as follows:

(a) **Avoidance:** When an individual uses this strategy he/she minimizes or denies that there are any symptoms to notice. Such individuals are believed to cope well with short term stress.

(b) **Confrontation:** Some individuals use the strategy of confrontation, especially to deal with stress; such individuals are believed to cope better with long term stressors.

(c) **Downward Comparison:** This strategy is used to cope with bad health news. Individuals who choose to do this compare their own situation to others who are worse off.

(d) **Personal Characteristics:** One's personal characteristics also considerably influences how one copes with stress. These include one's age, gender, sociocultural factors, educational level, experience in certain areas of life, etc. Two important personal characteristics that are most important are as follows:

- Culture
- Gender

With respect to culture, it has been observed that pain signifies different theories in different countries. There are gender differences in the development of certain illness as well as death, most of which is influenced by one's lifestyle choices also. In most cultures, especially USA, India, etc., women live longer than men. Men are also more likely to die in car accidents and homicides. Men are also exposed to more dangerous work environments and increased levels of stress. Men have higher rates of hypertension, ulcer, heart attacks and cancer, etc. They also have significantly shorter life experiences. One reason for this is that men are more preoccupied with work and external world and are less attentive to their bodies.

On the other hand, women experience more symptoms and have more physical ailments than men. Women for e.g., are more likelyto experience osteoporosis (a disorder of the bones, which become porous and brittle).

2. Seeking Help: Individuals do not seek help for all their problems. They are mostly selective and seek help only when they feel it is necessary to seek help. Some important points with respect to seeking help so as to cope with a given illness are as follows:

- We generally seek help, especially of a qualified practitioner, only when our symptoms become extreme.
- If people believe their symptoms have a psychological rather than a physical cause, they are more reluctant to go for help.
- If their complaints such as hemorrhoids or unplanned pregnancy or vaginal infection, etc., are embarrassing to talk about they may resist treatment.
- Individuals are also less likely to visit a physician if their ailment or symptoms are virus related or involves the upper half of the body.
- If people believe the benefits of going to a doctor are not worth the time and trouble of a visit, especially if the visit is not covered by medical insurance, they may hold back.
- People are also afraid of devastating or dangerous diagnosis and hence they avoid seeking help.

There are gender differences with respect to seeking help. Women generally are more sensitive to changes in their bodies and to pain and thus, visit a physician more often as compared to men. People generally make two common mistakes in deciding about going to a doctor:

(a) They may go too quickly or too often because we over interpret the seriousness of our physical ailments.

(b) They may ignore the symptoms of disease that should be treated at once Some examples of such disease/illness are as follows:

- A fever that is not obviously associated with a cold or stuffy nose.
- Signs of internal bleeding in the sputum, vomit or bowel movement.
- A persistent abdominal pain, especially when it is in one spot and associated with nausea.
- A stiff neck that is not associated with any physical strain or injury.

It should be remembered that many diseases are without illness, some these include:

- Hypertension
- Tuberculosis
- Heart diseases
- Anemia

Many individuals also do not seek help from qualified doctors because they find communication with them to be very difficult. It has been observed that doctors generally do not indulge in social and friendly conversation with patients. They use jargons and medical terminologies about which layman is not familiar. They also lack patience and communication skills of dealing with individuals who are poor, illiterate or irritating in their approach to illness. It has also been noted that female doctors spend more time with their patients, allow their patients to talk more so that more communication is exchanged and explain medical terminology better than male doctors.

3. Adhering To Treatment: Adhering to treatment requires taking medicines and prescribed treatment regularly and properly as advised by the physician. It has been estimated that more than 50 per cent of the adult patients do not follow or complete doctors prescribed treatment. Many factors influence whether an individual will adhere to treatment or not, some of which are as follows:

- Patients characteristics such as their age, educational level, etc.
- Nature of illness (e.g., HIV, diabetes, etc.).
- Treatment regimen (medication, exercise, etc.)

There are many reasons as to why people fail to adhere to a given treatment.

- Dissatisfaction with the physician is the most common reason for failure to adhere to a given treatment.
- Patients who have a warm or cordial relationship with their doctor and are involved in planning the treatment are more apt to comply with the doctors orders/advice.
- Patients who do not understand the nature of their illness or the instructions of the doctors are not likely to follow the treatment. It has been noted that when desired treatment is explained in everyday language with easy-to-follow written instructions, patients are much more likely to cooperate.
- Patient's beliefs about medication also influence adherence. Individuals, who worry about drug reactions, drug dependence, side effects of long term use of a given drug, etc., are least likely to take the medications as prescribed.
- The ways in which a message is framed also influences the adherence to treatment. A message can be framed either positively or negatively. A negatively framed message can be written like this "If you don't stop smoking, you are likely to die at a young age". A positively framed message would be something like this "If you stop smoking and do aerobic exercises, you will live longer". It has been observed, by experts, that positively framed messages from medical practitioners are best for promoting preventive behaviours, such as sticking to a healthy diet, whereas negatively framed messages are best for facilitating detection behaviours such as noticing a pain.

PROMOTING WELLNESS

Recent years have seen growing awareness about health and health related issues. Individuals in general have become more oriented towards maintaining good health. Once wellness was considered as absence of sickness, but today good health and wellness is viewed as more than the absence of a minor or major illness. Wellness can be defined as the positive ideal of health in which one strives to maintain and improve one's health. Optimum health is one that comes from:

- Good Genes
- Exercises
- Regular and periodic medical care.
- Avoiding health hazards such as smoking, drinking, etc.

Wellness can be promoted in wide variety of ways, some of which includes the following:

1. Taking charge of your own health
2. Eating sensibly
3. Getting enough sleep
4. Keeping physically fit
5. Finding social support

We would discuss each of these briefly.

1. Taking Charge of Your Own Health: Every individual must take charge of his/her own health. One should often be well informed and indulge in rational reasoning so as to take effective measures to improve wellness. Taking charge of your own health behavior means assuming greater responsibility for your own health. This can be achieved in following ways:

- Understanding how one's body works.
- Knowing how the body and mind interacts.
- Learning to manage stress effectively.
- Monitoring one's health.
- Getting periodic medical checkups.
- Keeping one's own medical records.
- Knowing the health risks related to one's family history.
- Being an active participant and decision maker with respect to one's own health care.

Each individual and his/her family should acquire information/knowledge about health and health issues from appropriate resources. Some important resources include:

- Qualified medical practitioners
- Community health officers

- Reading newspaper columns/articles, etc., about health issues, diet, illness, etc.
- Seeking help of elderly or knowledgeable persons such as nurses, qualified workers, etc.
- Internet resources and printed literature, pamphlets, etc.
- Seeking advice of family physician, etc.

Taking charge of one's health means learning how to relate to medical establishment. Research studies have shown that individuals are more likely to adhere to treatment plans when they feel they have control or decision making power over what happens to them medically. Individuals can take charge of one's health by becoming active participant in their health care. They have to be collaborative and cooperative with doctors and other medical personnel without surrendering their own rights.

2. Eating Sensibly: One of the best ways to promote wellness and good health is to eat sensibly. Eating sensibly involves both the amount and kind of food we eat. The amount of food is often measured in calories, which is a measurement of energy produced by food when oxidized or burned in the body. The number of calories needed each day depends on factors such as age, size and rate of metabolism. For e.g.,

- A woman in her early twenties with a desk job needs about 2000 calories in a day.
- A woman with a more active life needs about 2200 calories.
- A man with a desk job uses about 2500 calories.
- One with a fairly active job such as carpenter needs about 2800 calories.
- Men and women who are in strenuous jobs or in athletic training may need any where from 3000 to 4000 calories a day.

A well balanced diet includes adequate amounts of various groups of substances:

- Proteins
- Carbohydrates
- Certain fats
- Vitamins
- Minerals
- Fibers, etc

Bread, cereals, pasta provides complex carbohydrates which is a good source of nutrition and energy. Most overweight people consume too many carbohydrates in the form of high sugar foods. Proteins is found in meat and dairy products. These foods are relatively high in fat. One must also be concerned about the cholesterol in the food. Too much salt is harmful; especially it leads to high blood pressure.

3. Getting Enough Sleep: Not getting enough sleep may lead to health problems. Sleep deprivation has many detrimental consequences. Effects of sleep deprivation vary from one person to another. Sleep deprivation leads to the following effects: People deprived of sleep make greater errors on routine tasks and experience increased drowsiness, a strong desire to sleep and a tendency to fall asleep easily. Following important suggestions for overcoming sleep deprivation are worth noting:

- Go to bed and get up at about the same time each day.
- Before going to bed learn to relax, listen to music or practice yoga. Avoid strenuous exercise.
- Before sleeping, see that your bedroom is conditioned to sleep. Make sure that it is quiet and dark at a suitable temperature.
- Avoid alcohol and sleeping pills. These interfere with normal sleep cycle.

4. Keeping Physically Fit: Physical fitness can be defined as our ability to function efficiently and effectively including both health related and skill related fitness components. Physical fitness is the entire human organisms ability to function efficiently and effectively. Regular physical activity/exercise has number of advantages;

- Reduced risk of premature mortality.
- Reduced risk of coronary heart disease, hypertension, colon cancer and diabetes.
- It reduces depression and anxiety.
- Improves mood.
- Enhances ability to perform daily tasks throughout the life span.
- Physical fitness also provides us with a sense of mastery, helps us overcome sad moods and can even help fend off some forms of cancer.
- Physical fitness often inspires positive thoughts.

Physical Activity and Health Hazard: Physical activity has been associated with many health problems; some of which are as follows:

- Musculoskeletal injuries.
- Heart attack/sudden death. It generally occurs among sedentary people with advanced coronary disease who engage in strenuous activity to which they are unaccustomed.

Each individual has to establish his/her personal exercise program. Some important points related to such a program worth noting are as follows:

- Identify your personal physical fitness needs.
- Select personalized physical exercises to make exercises more enjoyable.
- Vary your activities, by varying your activities you can include areas that will develop different aspects of physical fitness.
- Exercise regularly. It is important that you perform your exercise to a level that will promote fitness usually a minimum of 20 to 30 minutes, three times a week.
- Periodically evaluate and modify your routine.

5. Finding Social Support: Social support from friends and family helps us to find comfort and advice. Some important points with respect to social support and wellness are as follows:

- It has been observed that individuals who are sociable are generally healthier than those who are not.
- It has been observed (Bishop 1994) that married people and those who live with others are healthier than individuals who live alone.
- Individuals who are socially isolated are at greater risk for health problems than those who are socially engaged.
- Social support is also related to fewer, sports injuries, decrease risk of heart disease in the elderly and better immune system functioning.

Questions

1. Write short notes on the following:
   (a) Body Image.
   (b) Psychological factors that influence physical illness.
   (c) Coping with illness.
2. Discuss the various ways for promoting wellness.

****

3 Taking Charge and Managing Motives and Emotions

In this chapter we would discuss the following four important topics:

1. Mastery and Personal Control.
2. Personal Resolve and Decision Making, Decision and Personal Growth.
3. Understanding Motivation.
4. Understanding Emotions.

Effective Adjustment requires achieving mastery and personal control as well as taking certain decisions concerning one's personal life. We would also discuss and understand how motivation and emotion influence our adjustment and personal growth.

MASTERY AND PERSONAL CONTROL

We often face dilemma in our life, especially with regard to personal control and decision making. If we perceive that a goal is attainable, we usually take charge (seek control) and surge into action. In other words we feel a sense of some control or personal mastery over our lives. On the other hand when we come across a situation where we are doubtful that a given goal is attainable, we are experiencing lack of control and are likely to avoid taking actions necessary to achieve the goal. Our perception as to whether we have mastery and control over a given situation considerably influences as to the type of decision we take in life.

Personal Control: The term personal control also means perceived control. It can be defined as the achieved amount of control we have over our lives. Some individuals want to achieve mastery over their lives and hence they learn to face important challenges in life, make certain choices and learn to adjust with it. Personal control and decision making associated with it plays a crucial role in our life and the life course that one would adopt.

Importance of Personal Control: Personal control has become very important today, for many reasons:

(i) Our lives are increasingly shaped by large impersonal bureaucracies, such as the government and business corporations, they have more impact on the economy than we do and thus influence our personal lives.

(ii) Personal control is also important because our lives today are considerably influenced by events or/and conditions beyond our immediate control such as economic recession, terrorism or hurricanes.

(iii) Civil rights movement, right to information and other such movements have taught us that individuals can gain greater mastery over their lives by active participation in the democratic process like participating in demonstrations and boycott or promoting certain pieces of legislation.

(iv) The independence that an average individual has acquired has made one realize that each of us has considerable power to shape our destinies through personal decisions and action such as-

- Choosing a career
- Choosing a place where to live
- Finding a marriage/life partner
- Changing our lifestyle and values, etc.

Perceived Control: One aspect of personal control is perceived control which can be defined as the belief that we can influence the occurrence of events in our lives. Personal control is very important because it appears to be one type of control that accounts for a motivation to behave in a certain fashion.

An important concept related to perceived control is Locus of Control which means the source from which an individual believe control over life events originates-either within the person (internal locus of control) or outside of the person (external locus of control) .

If you have perceived control, you are likely to benefit in many ways. Perceived control leads to:

- Improved well being.

- Better performance on various tasks.
- Better coping with adversity.

Those individuals who believe in external locus of control are more prone to depression and anxiety. Individuals who come from collectivist cultures such as Asia generally have external locus of control as compared to America where internal locus of control is highly valued.

Some other important differences with respect to perceived controls are summarized below:

- Men in general have a greater internal locus of control as compared to women, especially when older men and women are compared.
- People in developing countries perceive more externalized control than member of industrialized societies.
- Individuals from western cultures may prefer and have more experience with primary control whereas individuals reared in Asian cultures may prefer and experience secondary control.

Primary controls refers to actions directed at attempting to change the world to fit one's needs and desires. Secondary control involves the individual utilizing processes directed at making him or her fit into the world better.

Consequences of Perceived Control: Research studies have revealed that the presence or absence of perceived control or self mastery has important consequences in our lives, over and above the actual control available to us in a given situation. When we believe we can actually affect outcomes in our lives, choose amongst them, cope with the consequences and understand them we behave in a significantly different way than when we don't hold this belief. People who have perceived control tend to exhibit certain characteristics, as follows:-

(a) They are likely to seek knowledge and information about the events that affect their lives. They make greater efforts to acquire information about themselves and their environment. For example, when facing surgery or serious illness patients with a high degree of perceived control are especially

- Likely to seek information about their condition.
- To ask question to the doctors and nurses and

- To make use of resources available to them.

(b) People high in perceived control are likely to attribute responsibility to themselves and to their abilities and efforts rather than to luck or the environment, at least in regards to desirable outcomes.

(c) People high in perceived control are resistant to social actions that helps others.

(d) Individuals high in perceived control are strongly achievement oriented. They work harder at intellectual and performance tasks. They also achieve better grades as compared to those with less perceived control.

There is a strong positive relationship between perceived mastery or self control and personal adjustment. Individual's high in perceived control tend to:

- Be less anxious.
- Better adjusted.
- Less likely to be classified with psychiatric disorders.
- These individuals are also active, self-reliant.

The above mentioned qualities make such individuals more adjustment and growth oriented.

(e) People high in perceived control use effective strategies for coping with stress. Individuals high in perceived mastery tend to use positive coping strategies.

- Making a plan of action and sticking to it.
- Taking a step at a time.
- Taking professional help and doing what is recommended.

People low in perceived control are more apt to use maladaptive strategies, some of which are as follows:

- Wishing the problem would go away.
- Blaming themselves.
- Seeking relief through over reacting, drinking or abusing drugs.

Research studies have also revealed that the use of effective coping strategies promote better adjustment and growth.

(f) People high in perceived control are more likely to take steps that will maximize their health and well-being and minimize the risk of illness.

(g) People who have high perceived control think in ways that enable them to manage environmental demands in more effective ways. These individuals are especially:
- Apt to seek information about health maintenance
- Engage in preventive health practices.
- Adopt more positive attitudes about physical exercise.
- Participate in physical exercises more regularly.

(h) Individuals who have perceived control are:
- Likely to refrain from or give up the habit of smoking.
- To successfully, complete weight reduction programs.
- To co-operate with prescribed treatment for medical problems.

(i) High perceived self-control help to predict who will succeed in overcoming eating disorders and successfully recover from the trauma of heart attacks.

Misperception and Maladjustment: Many individuals misperceive personal control which often leads to maladjustment. Misperception of personal control usually tends to have negative consequences.

- Some individuals habitually believe that they have even less control over their lives than they really do and they prematurely surrender potential mastery available to them i.e., even if they can do certain tasks and situations they believe that they would not be in a position to do and hence would not make an attempt. Thus, loosing on the opportunity that is available to them.
- Some individuals believe that they have greater control than they actually do. This over optimistic belief leads to frustration and eventual disappointment.

In short mistaken beliefs about personal control leads to maladaptive behavior. Martin Seligman has done considerable work with regards to reduced personal control which he calls it as learned helplessness. According to Seligman psychological and physical difficulties such as unemployment, accidents, illness, death of spouse, terrorism, victimisation, etc., leads to feelings of learned helplessness. Learned helplessness is associated with variety of ills including:-

- Depression
- Academic failures

- Bureaucratic apathy and
- Premature death

Learned Optimism: One way in which we can achieve realistic perceived control is through learned optimism. Optimism helps individuals to acquire a sense of greater personal control over their lives, especially with respect to future events. Optimistic individuals have better adjustment. Learned optimism leads to the following advantages:

- Optimism is related to better problem solving under stress.
- Ego resiliency.
- Better physical health.
- Optimistic individuals indulge in active coping and seek social support when appropriate.

In learned optimism individuals learn to interpret life events in a reasonably accurate way to enhance our perceived control and thus our adaptive responses.

We learn to be optimistic during our childhood years. Parents can teach their children optimism by instructing them in problem solving skills and adaptive coping skills and by modeling optimistic thinking for their children.

Each individual has an explanatory style, which can be defined as the way in which we explain life events to ourselves. There are three main categories of explanatory style:

- Permanence (how long will the event last).
- Pervasiveness (how much does it affect me).
- Personalization (how much at fault am I?).

According to Seligman, optimism explanatory style tends to be appropriate in the following situation:

- If you are in a situation that involves achievement such as writing a research paper, getting promotion or winning a game, in such situation optimism helps.
- Optimism helps us to deals with situations involving stress.
- In situation where you want to inspire or gain people's confidence, it's better to use optimism.

Some important points with respect to optimism are as follows:

- If your goal involves planning for a risky and uncertain future, do not use optimism.

- If your goal is to counsel others whose future is dim, do not use optimism initially.
- If you want to appear sympathetic to people's troubles, do not start with optimism although once confidence and empathy are established, optimism may help.

PERSONAL RESOLVE AND DECISION MAKING

In our life we often have to take important decisions with respect to certain choices between various options. Decision making can be defined as the process of gathering information about relevant alternatives and making an appropriate choice.

The Process of Decision Making: Psychologist has developed a system far making wise decisions. In the process of decision making we go through the following stages:

(i) **Rise to the challenge:** In this stage we recognize a problem and attempt to over simplify a complete problem

(ii) **Search for alternatives:** In this stage we search for various alternative solutions to our problems. This stage requires attitudes of openness and flexibility.

(iii) **Evaluate the alternatives:** During this stage we evaluate various alternatives with regard to their practicality and consequences. In this stage we weigh various risks, costs and possible gains.

(iv) **Make a commitment:** During this stage we select one of the options. We generally choose an alternative that gives us maximum benefits at minimum costs.

(v) **Assess your decision:** Once we have taken a decision we can after some period of time assess it. We can assess our decision with respect to its quality, results and consequences. While assessing our decision we have to ask ourselves a few questions:

- Does your decision need review?
- Is it right to modify or change your decision?
- What behavior or attitudes you should adopt to make your decision satisfying?

No decision is a perfect decision. Hence, you should not over react with disappointment, criticism and self blame.

Behaviors Involved in Decision Making: In the process of decision making individuals indulge in certain behavior and cognitive processes, some of which are as follows:

(i) **Vigorous information processing:** In the earlier stages of decision making, individuals indulge in vigorous decision making. The process of vigorous decision making involves:
- Seeking out sources of information.
- Taking time to know and understand various sources of information.
- Talking to people who are in a position to help.

(ii) **Involvement of energy, emotions, etc.:** The process of gathering information is a time consuming process involving mental energy, disrupting routines and building tension and conflict, all of which can be unpleasant. Very often we take quick decision, make sharp judgments or use heuristics (i.e., decision which people in the same situation have used previously to solve their problems). We generally do not like people who are slow in decision making or who delay taking a decision. The tendency on the part of an individual to delay decision making is called as procrastination. Research studies have revealed that individuals who appear to procrastinate in decision making actually are more systematic and seek more information before they make a decision.

(iii) **Taking help of media:** In the process of decision making, many individuals use shortcuts and take help of media, especially the internet. The computer and the internet has become the number one source for health information for consumers. Media may not often give reliable information. The media can cause you to make mistake in your gathering and assessing information. Many individual regret after taking a particular decision because when taking a given decision they had not considered many facts about the said decision or that their decision was based on limited information.

(iv) **Post decisional regret:** A few individuals often regret after taking a given decision. Post decisional regret can be defined as the regret that is experienced shortly after an individual has taken a particularly difficult choice or decision. It is quite normal after you have made a decision to feel that you may have made an incorrect or poor decision and to experience regret. We all tend to suffer from the "grass is greener on the other side of the fence" phenomenon, but mostly after we make a decision. Post decisional regret generally occurs under the following conditions :-

- That the outcome is poorer than expected.
- Self blame for having made a bad decision.
- Missed opportunities, especially when the missed opportunity was a near miss.

Our actions tend to generate more regret in the short term while our inaction produces more regret in the long run. Similarly, people usually feel more regret because of inaction than from action.

(v) Cognitive dissonance and reactance in decision making: Cognitive dissonance is a state of imbalance between our thoughts, emotions and behavior. Whenever we experience regret over a given decision we experience cognitive dissonance i.e., discrepancy between our thoughts. Reactance can be defined as oppositional behavior we indulge in when others try to change us. Reactance occurs when others limit our personal freedom by getting us to do what they want us to do rather than what we want.

Making Better Decisions: Every individual is concerned with the question: How to make better decision? We can improve our decision making skills by taking into consideration the following suggestions:-

(i) Use sound judgment: We should make sound judgment. By sound judgment we mean drawing valid inferences from data. In order to make sound judgments we must ask ourselves some of the following questions-

- How common are the given facts?
- What are the various alternatives?
- How much the situational and chance factors influence your results?
- What are the specific practical implications of deciding and not deciding on a given issues, etc.?

(ii) Draw up a balance sheet: An individual taking a given decision must learn to draw a balance sheet of various alternatives listing the advantages and disadvantages of each course of action. It has been noted that balance sheet procedure helps them to make a comprehensive appraisal of a situation requiring a decision and promotes contingency planning i.e., what to do if something invalid or unexpected occurs? It has been also observed that people who use balance sheet procedure are more likely to stick to their decision and express fewer regrets about the options not taken.

(iii) Clarify your values and objectives: A decision maker has to clarify one's values and objectives. Many conflicts arise due to values. For example, conflict often arises when you want to choose between two opposing alternatives. Many students are caught between the conflict of different needs i.e., the needs to study, work, socialize and play.

(iv) Accept reasonable results: Do not be rigid or perfectionist in the decision making. There are no perfect decisions. Constant striving for perfection increases the probability of failure.

(v) Make the best of the faulty decision: We all make faults. Some individuals repeatedly make mistakes, few may make blunders. Do not try to shield yourself. Accept your mistakes/faults and make urgent and sincere efforts to correct your mistakes. Do not waste time in defending your faults. Do not substitute good reasons for valid reasons. Please learn from your mistakes and be ready to alter or modify your decision.

Decisions and Personal Growth: Many of the decisions that we take are crucial for one's personal growth, including overcoming problem behavior. Large numbers of individuals become struck in self defeating behavior because they have never made a decision to change their ways. We resist changes due to following reasons:

- Our past habit are strong and offer resistance for change.
- Psychological laziness.
- Fears and anxieties.
- Defensive behavior on our part.
- Inability to make a firm decision to change.

We can promote personal growth first by identifying the basic decision of our life and understanding where changes need to be introduced. In order to take decision for pesonal growth we must be prepared for:

- Changing our behavior.
- Modifying our attitudes and values.
- Overcoming negative, self defeating behavior.
- Be more committed and perseverant in your actions and follow-up.

- Increase your awareness about self as well as situations surrounding you.

In order to enhance personal growth, increase your self understanding, do not go by the trend or what majority of others do, do not listen to popular advices especially of lay persons. Consult expert and seek his/her opinion. Do not use short cuts and quick fixes. Take your own reasonable time. For example, if you are unable to decide about a particular course of study at present, doesn't matter. Take a break. Explore the various alternatives events to the extent of taking a drop for a year or two; instead of joining a wrong course and then, half way through the course, realizing that the said course is not meant for you. Many of our life choice are made in haste or under the influence of people whose interests rather than your own aptitude and liking are important.

Be prepared to reverse or change your decision if you want to really grow. For example, let us take the case of a 45 year old lawyer who married the daughter of a senior partner in his firm. He admitted to having married out of a mixed motive. That is although he had been genuinely attracted to his wife, he had also hoped that his connection would enhance his career. He soon discovered that conflict with his father-in-law complicated his life both at work and at home. Consultation with a specialist about his asthma attacks, which seemed worse during joint vacations at his in-law's summer home, suggested that the attacks were brought on by emotional conflict concerning his in-law. Gradually, the lawyer realized that it was not a good idea to marry the boss's daughter, so eventually he decided to start his own firm rather then divorce his wife. Although he went through a few lean years, soon had a flourishing law practice and was much happier in his marriage as well. Failure to make such a courageous decision often results in feeling of being trapped in one's career, or a dead end relationship, etc., and limits one's personal growth.

Decisions that enhance personal growth require one to change one's attitudes and the ways of looking at things.

UNDERSTANDING MOTIVATION

Motivation is derived from the word "motive". The word motive is derived from Latin word "Movere", which means to move or to energise. Motivation directs our behaviour to a particular goal by making us active. Motivation is generally defined as the force that energizes, directs, and sustains behavior. Motivation is an important energizing state of an organism. Motivation has to do with energizing and directing our efforts towards a meaningful goal. Our motivation is affected by many influences some of them rather obvious but others less so. The following table briefly distinguishes between motives and needs:

Motives	Needs
Motives are goal directed activities that energize and direct behavior.	Needs are tension states that arouse us to seek gratification.

Motivation and emotions are closely related to each other.

Understanding your needs: Our understanding of motivation can be enhanced by the study of Maslow's Hierarchy of Needs. Maslow divides needs into 5 basic levels such as:-

(i) Physiological needs including the need for food, sleep and sex.

(ii) Safety needs includes the need for protection from bodily harm and security from threat, as well as the needs for order and stability.

(iii) Love and belongingness needs include the need for acceptance, affection and approval.

(iv) Esteem needs are the need for self-respect and the sense of achievement.

(v) Self-actualizing needs include a variety of needs for-
- Autonomy
- Uniqueness
- Aliveness
- Beauty
- Justice, etc.

Some important points with respect to Maslow's hierarchy of needs are as follows:

- Fewer individuals have the top most needs (such as self-actualization) satisfied as compared to basic physiological needs.
- Lowest level of unmet needs remain the most urgent, thus commanding our attention and efforts.
- Maslow also pointed out that our needs typically remain

only relatively satisfied. He once estimated that the average person is only 85% satisfied in terms of physiological needs, 70% in safety needs, 50% in love needs, 40% in esteem needs and only 10% in self-growth needs. Therefore, he stated that there is constant motivation to meet needs.

- Need for competence, autonomy, self-determination, etc., are universal in nature.
- Our motives change over time depending on the motive targets around us. Motive targets are people towards whom our attention or motives are directed. For example, at work we have strong motives to compete with our associates (hence achievement, competence and power motivation may be in force at work place), In leisure hours we may be more concerned with being accepted by our friends (affiliation motive), At home we may feel inclined towards intimacy with our spouse, children, etc., (love motivation, maternal motivation, etc.).
- An individual's motive tends to vary across the entire life span and by culture, mostly because of one's experiences and personal growth.

Basic Needs: Basic needs include the need to eat, drink, sex, avoid extreme pain and injury, etc. Basic needs are also called as primary drives or survival motives. Our basic needs are influenced by the following factors:

- Parts of the brain, especially hypothalamus.
- Variety of learned influences.
- Cultural factors and value system.

Psychosocial Motives: Psychosocial motives refer to a group of motives that have less to do with physical survival and more to do with our sense of well being and psychological competence in dealing with our environment. Before we discuss the different types of psychosocial motives let us understand the concept of intrinsic and extrinsic motivation.

Intrinsic Motivation: It can be defined as an active engagement with tasks that people find interesting and that promotes growth. These tasks are freely engaged in out of interest. The aim of intrinsically motivated behavior is not to succeed or to reach some other outcome but rather to engage in an activity naturally and spontaneously. Such behaviors are inherently satisfying to pursue in and themselves.

Extrinsic Motivation: It is the desire to engage in activity because it is a means to an end and not because an individual is following his/her interest. Extrinsically motivated behaviors are not based on an individual's need to feel competent and autonomous but on some other external reward or outcome.

Large numbers of research studies carried out over the years have demonstrated that external rewards, surveillance, deadlines and threats undermine intrinsic motivation.

There is no authoritative list of what are psychosocial motives. The most common are as follows:

(i) Stimulation needs which includes the motives for stimulation, curiosity and exploration. These needs are largely inborn.

(ii) Achievement motives is the most important Psychosocial motive which is shaped largely by psychological, cultural and social influences.

(iii) Other motives are friendship need, sexual motivation, need for personal freedom and control, etc.

We would discuss stimulation motive and achievement motive in brief:

Stimulation Motive: Stimulation motivation includes sensory as well as social stimulation. These needs are generally deprived among the following group of individuals

- Prisoners in solitary confinement.
- Subjects in sensory deprivation experiments.
- Military personnel in lonely outposts.

Research studies have revealed that sensory and social stimulation deprivation among individuals leads to symptoms of stress, including distorted perceptions such as hallucination, delusions and fear of loosing one's sanity.

Marvin Zuckerman has introduced the concept of Sensation Seeking Motive. It is the motive to seek out stimulating and novel experiences. Our sensation seeking motive is partly dependent on biological factors such as brain stimulation and biochemical secretions (especially Dopamine).

A study of college students (Hansen and Breivik, 2001) found that those high in sensation seeking motive took more trials, both positive (e.g., Kayaking) and negative (e.g., Shop lifting). Higher score is also highly correlated with more drug use.

Sensation Seeking influences our perception of others and the ways in which we relate to one another. Low sensation seekers may feel that high sensation seekers are foolhardy and hungry for attention. In contrast; high sensation seekers may feel that low sensation seekers are timid and boring.

Achievement Motivation: Achievement Motivation is also called as the Need for Achievement (n Ach) and is one of the most important psychological motives. David McCelland, Atkinson and Litwin have done considerable work on the need for achievement. McCelland has observed that need for achievement is related to economic growth. Societies with a high need for achievement have a high rate of economic growth than societies with a low need for achivement. It is the desire to accomplish or master something difficult or challenging as independently and successfully as possible. It is concerned with setting goals and achieving them. It is concerned with becoming successful in whatever activity one undertakes and avoiding failures. People with a strong achievement motive not only like to excel others, but also try to do better than what they did in the past. Individuals who are high in need for achievement do better in school, in their job and in other areas of life. People with a strong achievement motive choose tasks, which are neither very easy nor very difficult but the one which they are confident of accomplishing through their best efforts.

Two important elements of achievement motivation are as follow:

(a) Desire for success
(b) Fear of failure

Our achievements motivation is influenced by wide variety of factors. The most important is self-efficacy which can be defined as the belief in one's capabilities to organize and execute the course of action required to produce given attainments.

Personal Motivation: Personal motivation has to do with setting personal goals. Many of us do not set such goals and go around our life without any agenda. By not setting personal goals we waste considerable degree of time and energy. There are many types of personal goals, somc of which are listed below:

(i) **Long range goals:** These are concerned with the kind of life you want to live with regards to your career, marriage, lifestyle, etc.

(ii) **Medium range goals:** These include goals set for next 5 years or so such as planning to get married or complete higher studies, etc. Most individuals generally have control over these goals and can tell as to how well you are progressing towards them.

(iii) **Short range goals:** These goals cover a period ranging from next one month up to a year. Short range goals can be set easily. We should strive hard to achieve these goals.

(iv) **Mini goals:** These goals cover anything from one day to a month. We generally have control over these goals. We should try to make these goals highly specific.

(v) **Micro goals:** These goals cover a period of next 15 days to a few hours. You have direct control over these goals.

It should be remembered that the shorter the time span covered, the more control we have over our goals.

UNDERSTANDING EMOTIONS

Emotion is one of the most important aspects of our behaviour. The term emotion is derived from the latin word "emovere" meaning 'to move out' or 'to excite'. The term emotion is also used interchangeably with the term affect.

Emotion can be defined as a complex state involving feelings, expressions, physiological changes that have the power to motivate us.

Emotions can be defined as complex pattern of changes that includes physiological arousal, subjective feelings, cognitive processes and behavior reactions.

Components of Emotions: The four most important components of emotions are as follows:

(i) **Physiological arousal:** Emotion includes physiological changes associated with brain, nervous system and hormones.

(ii) **Subjective feelings:** It includes elements of pleasure or displeasure, liking or disliking. Subjective feelings can best be understood by relying on individual's self reports.

(iii) **Cognitive processes:** It includes memories, perception, expectation and interpretations. Our appraisal (i.e., evaluation or interpretation) of an event plays an especially significant role in the meaning it has for us.

(iv) Behavior reactions: Emotions involves two types of behavior reactions:

- Expressive
- Instrumental

Expressive reactions include facial expression, gestures, tones of voice, etc. These reactions serve to communicate our feelings to others. Instrumental reactions include cries of distress and running for our lives.

Research studies have revealed that for healthy adjustment it is better to have a target repertoire of emotions and duty to call on each where appropriate.

Experiencing Emotions: We experience wide variety of emotions. Some emotions are intense others are mild.

- Intense emotions tell us our lives are strongly affected by some person or event and prompt us to act accordingly.
- Not feeling any emotion in a situation where we should experience certain emotion is a sign of maladjustment or abnormality.
- Our emotions are in a state of constant flux or change so that we may feel pleased at one moment and annoyed the next.
- We experience both primary as well as secondary emotions. Plutchik identified eight different types of primary emotion: Joy, acceptance, fear, surprise, sadness, disgust, anger, anticipation. These emotions can be experienced more or less intensely to create other emotions.

Emotions have also been classified in to following two categories.

1. **Pleasant v/s unpleasant emotions:** Emotion of contentment, joy and love fall into the category of pleasant emotion. Anger, disgust and sadness fall into the category of unpleasant emotions.
2. **Intensely v/s weakly aroused emotions:** Some emotions are strongly aroused in us whereas others are weakly aroused. The strength of the emotion is influenced by many factors including many cognitive variables.

Expressing Emotions: Individuals differ with respect to how they express emotion. Expression of emotion is considerably influenced by many factors. These include:

- Physiological states, biochemical, neuroauromatic conditions, etc.
- Gender
- Cultural factors

Some important points with respect to expressing emotions that are worth noting are as follow:

(i) There are gender differences in the expression of emotions.

(ii) In wide variety of cultures men more frequently report powerful emotions (for e.g., Anger) while women are more likely to report powerless feeling (for e.g., Fear).

(iii) Researchers have consistently found that women are better decoders than are men of other's emotions, especially of body postures.

(iv) Men, more than women ruminate about upsetting events and report more inhibition of hostile feelings.

(v) Older persons rehearse more about upsetting events and express emotions less frequently than younger individuals.

(vi) Culture plays an important role in expression of emotions. For e.g., Japanese – Americans report the lowest expressiveness in romantic relationship. Asians report the lowest intensity of positive emotions.

(vii) Many important parts of the body listed below signal to us what others are actually feeling. These are
   - Body postures.
   - Vocal changes (e.g. Pitch modulation and speed of speech).
   - Hand gestures, etc.

(viii) Some individuals can deceive others through deceptively manipulating one's facial expressions.

Two important aids to detecting deception through facial expressions are as follows:

(a) Micro expression: These are fleeting facial expressions that last only a fraction of a second. Micro expression can be ephemeral, but they are still detectable by the astute observer.

(b) **Body leakage:** A phenomenon in which body postures rather than face leak the truth, especially about emotional deceit.

Managing Emotions: Psychological adjustment requires learning to manage one's emotions appropriately. Learning to express feelings effectively involves a suitable balance between spontaneous expression and deliberate rational self regulation. You have to learn to express your feelings openly and in constructive manner. One method of expressing intense emotions, introduced by Tom Gordan, is ***'I' message***. This message consists of saying what you honestly feel in a way that encourages other to listen and co-operate. "I" message are especially helpful in expressing your feelings about someone whose behavior has become a problem for you. "I" message consist of four components.

(i) First describe the other person's objectionable behavior in specific but non-judgmental terms. Avoid using furry and accusatory responses or guessing the person's motives. Such communication only intensifies the person's resistance to changing the behavior.

(ii) Point out the specific ways in which that person's behavior affects you. In most instance, people are not deliberately trying to make life miserable for you, they simply aren't aware or the consequences of their actions. Once a person becomes more aware of how his behavior has become a problem for you, the person is usually willing to modify it.

(iii) Tell the person how you feel about the behavior in a way which makes you responsible not the other person. For e.g., say "I feel hurt" instead "you hurt me". Avoid projecting your emotions on the other person.

(iv) Finally, tell the person what you have done to correct the situation.

Special Emotions: Some important emotions that we experience in our daily life and that influence our adjustment are as follows:

1. Anxiety
2. Anger
3. Jealousy
4. Happiness

We would discuss each of these briefly

1. Anxiety: It can be defined as a vague pleasant feeling that serves as an emotion's alarm signal, warning us of an impending threat or danger. In the ancient times anxiety was largely a result of:

- Natural disasters
- Danger from predators
- Interclan hostilities, etc.

Today we often experience anxiety as a result of the following:

- Frustration
- Bureaucracies
- Personal achievements and failure
- Non-life threatening issues, such as loss of job; break up in romantic relationship, etc.

Anxiety has many detrimental causes with respect to adjustment. Some important points with respect to adjustment and anxiety are as follows:

- Moderate levels of anxiety may motivate us to take necessary steps to avoid gaffe (blunder).
- Free floating anxiety may make a given situation worse.
- High levels of anxiety can distort our perception and thinking so much that our performance is impaired.
- Anxiety siphons off energy by keeping us mobilized for actions when none is required. It makes us tense and tired-thereby robbing us of much of the enjoyment of life.

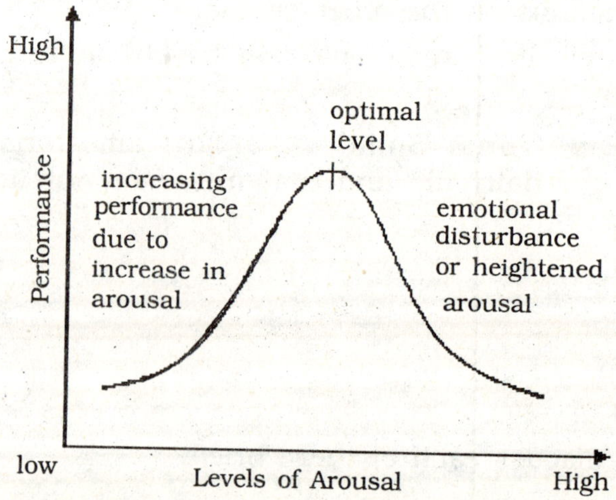

Some of the most common types of anxieties experienced by individuals are as follows:

- Math's and computer related anxiety.
- Anxiety associated with the social situations.
- Anxiety associated with evaluation, performance appraisal, exams, interviews, etc.,

One special type of anxiety is test anxiety. It has been observed that test anxiety hinders performance.

Relationship Between Anxiety and Performance: Generally the relationship between anxiety and test performance takes the form of an inverted U curve. The inverted "U" hypothesis states that as the test anxiety (levels of arousal) increases, performance also increases but only to an optimal degree, beyond this optimal degree, any further increase in test anxiety would lead to decline in the performance on a test. The inverted U relationship between test anxiety and performance was demonstrated by Hebb and also by Yerkes and Dodson.

Three important findings with respect to relationship between anxiety and performance are as follows:

- Low level of anxiety is associated with unmotivated behavior; such individuals perform well only on easy, not difficult tasks.
- Moderate levels of worry tend to enhance performance, at least up to a point.
- High levels of anxiety lead to distraction and the consequent result is poor performance.

What is an optimal level of anxiety? Difficult to answer. Individuals differ with respect to their optimal levels of anxiety.

2. Anger: It can be defined as feeling of displeasure or resentment over (perceived) mistreatment. An important question concerning anger is whether you should hold and suppress your anger or should you vent out your anger. It has been observed that holding anger in, leads to all kinds of problems such as:

- High blood pressure
- Increased risk of heart attack
- Depression
- Suicide, etc.

Venting out one's aggression/anger is called as Catharsis. It has been observed, in many experimental studies, that displacing anger onto more productive projects is an effective strategy to manage one's anger. It has been observed that people who suppress or hold in their high levels of anger are more prone to high blood pressure and heart attacks. An important syndrome related to this is "type A" and "type B" personality characteristics.

Research studies have revealed that effective management of anger is possible. Some important strategies for effectively managing anger are as follow:

(i) Child rearing practices helps to prevent inappropriate forms of anger expression.

(ii) Parents should display appropriate anger management techniques. Children often imitate parents. Parents should

- Avoid shaming a child's anger.
- Increase a child's understanding of anger.
- Help a child to achieve sense of control over anger arousing events.
- Encourage sense of control over anger arousing events, by inculcating secure attachment. Securely attached children have parents whom they love and trust and want to emulate.
- Do not expose your child to aggressive models. See to it that child does not watch aggressive acts on television. There is much evidence that watching televised violence desensitizes us to its effects.
- Parents should be cautious about physically punishing their children, especially when the child has temper tantrum or has acted aggressively towards another. Such parents are modeling the very behavior they are trying to eliminate in their children.
- Training in social skills can also help the child or others in controlling their anger.

3. Jealousy: It is a complex emotion that occurs when we fear losing a close relationship with another person or have lost it already. Jealously is often contrasted with envy which can be defined as feelings of inferiority, longing, resentment and disapproval. Some important features of jealousy with respect to adjustment are as follows:

- Jealousy is characterized by fear of loss, distrust, anxiety and anger.

- Jealousy is especially apt to occur in romantic and sexual relationship, such jealousy is also called as romantic jealousy. It can be normal or pathologic.

Some important situations that are likely to trigger jealousy are as follows:

- The person you like goes out with someone else.
- Someone gets closer to a person to whom you are attracted.
- Your lover/spouse tells you how sexy a former boyfriend/girlfriend was.
- Your lover/spouse visit a person. He/she used to go out with.
- You find your partner is having an affair.
- Your spouse/mate has to pay maintenance to his/her previous spouse.

Some individuals are more prone to jealousy; such individuals have the following characteristic:

- Low self esteem
- High levels of anxiety
- A negative view towards the world
- Low levels of life satisfaction
- Little control over their lives
- Low threshold of emotional arousal
- Greater sensitivity to threatening stimuli in social environments

4. Happiness: It is also called as Subjective Well- Being (SWB). It can be defined as preponderance of positive thoughts and feelings about one's life. People high in SWB have the following characteristic:

- Subjective satisfaction that one's work, marriage and other life domains are satisfactory.
- Those high in SWB experience and report pleasant rather than anxious, angry or depressive emotions.
- Happy people are less self-focused, less hostile and less vulnerable to disease.
- Happy people are more loving, forgiving, trusting, energetic, decisive, creative, helpful and sociable as compared to people who are unhappy.

- Happy people have high self esteem, a sense of personal control, optimism and extroversion.
- Happy people often loose a sense of time and self because they find a task challenging and absorbing.

Questions

1. Discuss how Mastery and Personal Control influence one's Adjustment.
2. Write short notes on the following:
   (a) Learned Optimism
   (b) The Process of Decision Making
   (c) Behaviours Involved in Decision Making
   (d) Decisions and Personal Growth
3. Write a note on Understanding Motivation.
4. Write a note on Understanding Emotions.
5. Write short notes on the following:
   - Various Components of Emotions
   - Special Emotions and the process of Adjustment

****

4 Making and Keeping Friends

MEETING PEOPLE

Friendship is one of the most central aspects of our life and relationships. Some friendships last forever, others are short lived and most friendships are nothing more than short term acquaintances. With friends we share secrets, troubles and joys. Those who lack close friendship often experience emotional isolation and loneliness, regardless of their network of other acquaintances. In this section we will discuss following topics:

1. Are first impressions most important?
2. Mistaken impressions
3. Shyness

We would discuss each of these topics in brief.

1. Are first impression most important? Whenever we encounter an individual for the first time, we form first impression about him/her which often influence our subsequent interactions. First impression can be defined as the initial impressions we form of others in which we tend to judge them on the basis of very little information. Forming the first impression is very natural and inescapable process.

When forming the first impression we do not treat all incoming information equally. Negative and positive information are assessed differently.

- While forming first impression, negative information is given more weight and remains more stable.
- We expect others to form positive first impression. Hence, whenever we are meeting an individual for the first time we need to use impression management techniques to

impress that person so that he/she may form positive impressions about us.

- First impressions are generally indelible i.e., they are relatively permanent. Our subsequent impressions or interactions are considerably influenced or colored by the first impression that we have formed about others.

Many factors influence our first impressions about others, some of which are as follows;

(i) Physical attractiveness

(ii) Reputations

(iii) Similarity

(iv) Propinquity

(v) Non-verbal signs and

(vi) Verbal signs

We would discuss each of these briefly.

(i) Physical attractiveness: An individual's physical features considerably influence the ways in which we form impressions about others. Some important points with respect to physical attractiveness and impression formation are as follows:

- The more physically attractive someone is, the more positively we analyze that person.
- When individuals are told to give impression of others, they attribute all sorts of positive qualities to attractive people.
- Attractive people are judged to be more interesting, intelligent, compassionate, sociable and better adjusted than less attractive person.
- Attractive people are regarded as more successful in their careers and happier in their lives. Physical attractiveness has been found to be positively correlated with following accomplishments:

  (a) Earning better grades.

  (b) Having better jobs.

  (c) Obtaining faster promotions.

  (d) Having less serious psychological disorders.
- Individuals are ethnocentric while judging members of their own group on attractiveness. It has been observed that individuals find members of their own group more attractive as compared to members of other groups.

- One important concept related to physical attractiveness is **Matching Hypothesis:** Each of us may fantasize about having a highly attractive romantic partner. In reality, when it comes to choosing a date or romantic partner, we usually settle for someone like ourselves, at least in regard to physical attractiveness. This tendency has been labeled as matching hypothesis. Thus, matching hypothesis refers to the idea that people are more likely to form successful relationships with and express liking for people whose level of physical attractiveness roughly equals their own. Example: A man of average attractiveness goes on one date with an extremely attractive person, and then another with an average-looking person. He finds he likes the average-looking date more.
  - Unattractiveness is often judged unfavorably. Unattractiveness is highly subjective term. For e.g.:
  - For some people obesity or homely facial features appears to be ugly.
  - For others features such as irregular large nose, discolored skin or physical handicap may be ugly.
  - For still others deviations from accepted norms may be sign of ugliness.

Unattractive people are discriminated against for no good reason.

It was Berscheid et.al., (1971) who with respect to physical attractiveness stated the matching hypothesis. It states that individuals are attracted to one another as friends, romantic partners or spouses on the basis of similar attributes-physical attractiveness, age, race, personality characteristics, or social assets such as wealth, education, or power. Thus, matching hypothesis means that each of us may desire the most physically attractive person to be our mate but when it comes to actual choosing we choose the one which we feel we could get, i.e., the one who is more or less equal to us in physical attractiveness. Such matching is not simply a feature of campus romances but the same tendency influences casual dates, engagements and marriages (Murstein, 1972). Married couples regardless of their age or length of marriage are similar in attractiveness. Even same sex friends tend to resemble each other in attractiveness and this is true for both males and females.

(ii) Reputations: An individual's reputation considerably influences our first impressions about him/her.

(iii) Similarity: Similarity is another important factor that influences how we form first impressions about others. Some important points with respect to similarity and adjustment are as follows:

- Research has shown that there is strong correlation between liking and similarity.
- People with the same attitudes are attracted to one another "Birds of a feather flock together".
- Research studies by Byrne et.al., (2004) has revealed that "the higher the proportion of similar attitudes between the people, the more they like each other".

(iv) Propinquity: Propinquity refers to physical closeness between two friends, Generally people who become friends are the one who lived nearby, attended same school or worked at same place. It has been observed that geographic nearness is especially important in the early stages of attraction. Many studies have demonstrated that the farther away the person lives or sits (in class, for e.g.) the less likely that person is to become a friend.

A large body of research studies has shown that the closer two people live the more likely they are to be "best friends" as opposed to simply good friends. Repeated exposure is an important factor influencing interpersonal attraction. Repeated exposure is defined as a frequent contact with a stimulus person. Long ago Zajonc (1968) found that repeated exposure to a new stimulus, such as a stranger's face, or abstract drawing or a given product, etc., results in an increasing positive evaluation of that stimulus.

(v) Non-verbal signals: Other's non-verbal facial expressions and features also play an important role in attracting us towards them. Our impressions of others are shaped by variety of non-verbal signals:

- In general, if a new acquaintance's face or gestures remind us of someone else's that we knew and like, we transfer our positive feelings about the old acquaintance to the new one.
- On the other hand, we also tend to transfer our negative feelings about a disliked person onto a new acquaintance who remind us about a disliked person.

- Similarly, those who walk youthfully make more favorable impression than those who are slow.
- Similarly, people who point, glare and interrupt a lot, make more negative impression than those who are attentive to what we say.
- We are favorably impressed with people who smile and look us in the eye. People who make eye contact with us are apt to be seen as more trustworthy and likeable unless they gaze into our eyes for an uncomfortably long time.
- Those whose faces appear angular seem to be more threatening or angry while whose faces appear rounded are perceived to be happy and likeable.

(vi) Verbal signals: Our impression about others is also shaped by other people's verbal communication patterns, especially, the rate of speech, pauses and pitch. These unspoken but important features of spoken communication are called as paralinguistics. The use of paralinguistic cues in interpersonal communication has been greatly reduced by e-mail and internet.

2. Mistaken Impressions: Mistaken impressions are false or erroneous perceptions of others, often based on insufficient evidence. We have mistaken impressions of others because of lack of sufficient information about them. Some important phenomenons related to mistaken impressions are as follows:

(a) Heuristics: They are mental shortcuts that people use for making complex decisions. Heuristics are simple decision making rules we often use to make inferences or draw conclusions quickly and easily. In other words, heuristics are simple rules for making complex decision or drawing complex inferences in a rapid manner. We make use of many mental heuristics in our effort to think about and use social information.

(b) False Consensus Effect: It is one of type of heuristics in which we assume others feel as we do. The false consensus effect is a tendency to assume that others behave or think like we do to a greater extent than is actually true. In false consensus effect we assume that other think as we do, and would agree with us, to a greater extent than they really do. False consensus effect has been observed in numerous contexts. For example, male high school students who smoke estimate that 51 percent of their fellow male students smoke, but non-smoking male students estimate that only 38 percent of their male peers smoke (Shemian et. al., 1984). In a similar manner, students tend to overestimate the proportion of other students who agree with their attitudes about drugs, abortion, seat-belt use, university policies and politics.

(c) **False Cues:** It consists of various signals and indirect suggestion that unconsciously trigger certain associations in our minds. Because people who are successful and financially well off frequently live in large, impressive houses and drive expensive cars, we assume mistakenly that anyone who indulges in expensive cars and clothes is rich.

(d) **Stereotypes:** We also misjudge people because of stereotypes. These are widespread generalizations that have little, if any, bases in fact and typically are held about groups and people. Whenever people begin statements with phrases such as "all teachers" or "women drivers" or "these people are all the same" they are slipping into stereotypical thinking. Stereotypes can be defined as cognitive frameworks consisting of knowledge and beliefs about specific social groups and the typical or "modal" traits supposedly possessed by persons belonging to these groups. Stereotype refers to the belief that all members of a specific social group share certain traits or characteristics. Stereotypes are cognitive frameworks that strongly influence the processing of incoming social information. Information that is relevant to a particular stereotype is processed more quickly than information not related to it. Information inconsistent to our stereotype is filtered out through reasoning and argument but information consistent with stereotype is processed without reason

Some of the most common stereotypes are as follows:

- People who wear glasses are smarter than those who don't.
- Men with beards, mustaches and abundance of body hair are more masculine and virile than those with less hair.
- Brunette Women are seen as more intelligent and responsible than blondes.
- Redheads of both sexes are seen as more "hot tempered" then people with other hair colors.

(e) **Halo v/s Devil Effect:** We often tend to label people as "good" or "bad" on the basis of the few traits they possess. This phenomenon is called either halo or devil effect. Halo effect is inferring uniformly positive traits from the appearance of a few positive traits. Devil or Horns effect means inferring negative traits from an appearance of a few negative traits.

(f) **Fundamental Attribution Error:** The Fundamental Attribution Error is defined as a strong tendency to explain other's actions in terms of dispositional (internal) rather than situational (external) causes. In short, we tend to perceive others as acting as they do because they are that kind of person rather than because of the many situational factors. Thus, the fundamental attribution error can be defined as the tendency to over estimate the impact of dispositional causes on other's behaviour. We often misjudge other people by not taking sufficient account of situational influences on their behaviour. We assume that people are always acting in character (i.e. behavior is trait induced). For e.g., if you drop a cup of tea, others present around you would think of you as clumsy rather than attribute the spill to the fact that coffee was hot. The tendency to attribute people's behavior to their personalities rather than to their circumstances is called a fundamental attribution error. In order to understand individual's true nature it is wise to observe someone in a variety of different situations across time in order to know what that person is really like.

3. Shyness: It can be defined as the tendency to avoid contact or familiarity with others. It is also defined as the fear of social reflection and social incompetence. Shyness can be defined as discomfort, inhibition and excessive caution in interpersonal relationship. It has been found to be highly correlated with loneliness. Shyness is not a general personality trait but is situational specific. This means that only certain situations lead to shyness. Zimbardo (1990) identified the following characteristics of shyness:

- Timid about expressing themselves.
- Overly self-conscious about how others are reacting to them.
- Get embarassed easily.
- Experience physiological symptoms of anxiety.

According to one estimate (Carducci 1999, Marano 2005) almost half of all Americans report a chronic problem of shyness. Similarly, about 80% of college going students report they have been shy, at some point in their lives. Shyness is typically consistent across spheres, to be an enduring personality trait.

Social Phobia: One type of shyness is social anxiety or social phobia.

Overcoming Shyness: Shyness can be overcome through the following steps.

(i) Strive to reduce the inner monitoring of your own thoughts, feelings and actions, especially the concern for how people see you and whether they will reject you. Instead focus on your participation in the activity.

(ii) Identify those aspects of the situation that elicit shyness, such as meeting new people, the social skills that you may be lacking, etc.

(iii) Develop a few social skills, such as how to initiate and carry on a conversation, how to assert yourself, etc.

(iv) Shyness subsides when you step out of your usual identity i.e., "I am a professor", "I am only student", "I am a women", etc.

(v) Avoid being self-critical and perfectionist.

KEEPING FRIENDS

If making new friends is a difficult task, then keeping old friends or friends already made is much more difficult. Forming friendship and the desire for human connectedness and attachment is a fundamental human motive. In this section we will discuss following topics.

1. Friendship
2. When friends get together i.e., social support
3. Self-disclosure
4. Same sex, opposite-sex friends
5. Staying friends
6. Loneliness

We would discuss each of these briefly.

1. Friendship: It can be defined as affectionate attachment between two or more people. Friendship has to do with the quality of the relationship rather than with the frequency of association. High quality of friendship has the following characteristics:

- Helping one another.
- Intimacy or disclosing of secrets.
- Mutual praise for success.
- Loyalty.

Close friendship can save us from depression and loneliness and thus enhance our mental and social wellbeing.

2. When Friends Get together? What do friends do when they get together? One of the most common activities among friends is having an intimate talk. This is one of the activities most frequently mentioned by men, women and children. One type of support offered by friends especially during stress is called as Social Support. It can be defined as a process whereby one individual or group offers comfort and advise to others who can use it as a means of coping.

3. Self-disclosure: Self-disclosure can be defined as sharing of intimate or personal information with others. As the relationship between two people progresses from strangers to acquaintances to close friends, individuals disclose a greater breadth and depth of information about themselves. Large number of research studies demonstrates that self-disclosure, especially of personal secrets has health benefits.

4. Same-sex, Opposite-sex Friends: There are gender differences in friendship. Some important points with respect to gender differences in friendship are as follows:

- Intimacy plays a more central role among women friends.
- Women generally are more physically and emotionally expressive in their friendships than men.
- Women are more apt to share intimate details about their lives, such as their worries, joys, secrets, etc.
- Women experience greater anxiety over close relationships. Tensions, jealousies and rejections are more common in friendship between women.
- Men engage in outright disputes over money, property and dominance.
- Men are not emotionally as close in their friendships with other men.

One of the important questions with respect to opposite-sex friend is, can you be a close friend with someone of the opposite sex without being romantically or seriously involved with this person?

5. Staying Friends: Many of us value old friends, because with old friends we can relax and be ourselves without much fear of rejection. Staying friends depends more on the special qualities of the relationship and less on the frequency of contact between two people.

Class reunions and vacations provide us with opportunities for reviewing old ties.

Friendship break-up due to many reasons, some of which are as follows:

(i) The most common reason as to why people breakup in life is transitions. In fact 77% of Americans adults revealed that friendships ended due to life changes such as marriage, child-birth, new jobs, etc.

(ii) Friendships also ended when trust was broken or when you were betrayed by friends i.e., when trust was broken. Trust can be defined as people's abstract positive expectations that they can count on friends and partners to care for them and be responsive to their needs, now and in the future.

(iii) Friendship may also break off because the individuals discover they have very different views on matters that are important to them.

6. Loneliness: It can be defined as a subjective state reflecting the fact that the quality and quantity of relationship wanted is lower than the quality and quantity of relationship available. Loneliness can be defined as a subjective feeling of distress, which occurs when an individual has fewer interpersonal relationships than desired or when these relationships are not satisfying as desired.

Loneliness should not be confused with solitude which is more objective and often a desired state denoting the absence of people. You can feel lonely despite being surrounded by others if you are not close to those people. Loneliness can be associated with depression, anxiety, unhappiness and shyness. Lonely individuals tend to smoke more, have more sedentary lifestyle and are more obese than those who are socially connected.

Factors contributing to loneliness:

- People who have grown up with warm and helpful parents (i.e., securely attached to their parents) are less likely to report loneliness in adulthood than those who describe their parents as disagreeable and unhelpful.
- Some of the loneliest people are those whose parents are divorced when they were younger then 6 years old, partly because younger children misperceive parental divorce as abandonment. In contrast people who have lost parents through death experience no corresponding increase in loneliness, probably, because they realize that the loss was not intentional or due to their fault.
- People who have low self-esteem and reduced social skills experience more loneliness as compared to those who have high self-esteem. Individuals with low self-esteem are lonely because their beliefs in their own unworthiness limit their reflection of positive feedback from others. These individuals have reduced emotional intelligence, which can be defined as the ability to regulate one's own actions
- Recent research studies have also revealed that loneliness and culture are correlated. The emphasis on personal fulfillment, often at the expense of subtle relationships and commitment to others, is thought to make individuals especially prone to loneliness.

Coping with Loneliness: There are many ways of dealing with loneliness and adjusting to it. How well we cope with loneliness depends largely on how we interpret its causes. Some important points with respect to overcoming loneliness are as follows:

(a) People who suffer most from loneliness tend to exaggerate its internal aspects and minimize its external ones. For e.g., some people blame their loneliness on their personal inadequacies such as "I am lonely because I am unlovable" or "I and my lover have split because I gained too much weight and became unattractive to him". Such a feeling often leads to loneliness and increases one's depression. One of the best ways to overcome loneliness is to emphasize on the external aspects of the situation and not to exaggerate the internal aspects.

(b) People are more likely to overcome their loneliness when they focus on the external, situational factors that contribute to it. Such as "It is hard to meet people in large classes", "I will find some time to socialize and meet new people....either by joining a health club or lion's club, etc."

(c) People who react to loneliness in passive ways such as watching a television, crying and sleeping – feel even lonelier. Those who adopt more active or behavioural strategies, such as writing a letter or calling up an acquaintance are more likely to alleviate their loneliness.

(d) Developing certain social skills, especially interpersonal skills as well as changing one's cognitive framework also plays an important role in overcoming loneliness.

Overcoming Loneliness: Some important steps to overcome loneliness are as follows:

(i) **Use of Internet:** Internet is one of the best ways to help an individual overcome loneliness. On Internet you can only seek a good deal of information from different sites as well as form friendship and interact with others. One of the greatest dangers is that if you spend considerable time on the Internet and online relationship, you will not have enough time to indulge in face-to-face communication; this may isolate you and lead to enhanced loneliness.

(ii) **Look out for opportunities for interaction with others:** Lonely individuals have been found to indulge more in activities like listening to music and reading in order to overcome their loneliness. This is no doubt a good strategy for overcoming loneliness, but it does not help them to develop "real world" friendship. Lonely individuals should develop the skill of forming new friendship. Most lonely individuals have been found to have avoidant attachment styles. They must learn to interact with people. They can become members of some social or welfare club, join classes or attend social functions, which will bring them in touch with people and lead to friendly interactions.

(iii) **Overcome self-defeating attribution style:** Lonely individuals must learn to overcome self-defeating attribution style. They should learn positive self-talk such as "I known my conversational skills are weak, but I will learn to develop them". Another positive style would be "It is difficult to find a good compatible partner but I will keep on searching till I find one". Another good attribution style would be "No one is perfect, even though I make mistakes I will try to improve every time and move more and more towards perfection". These above mentioned attribution styles would help an individual to adopt a positive interaction styles and help him or her to overcome loneliness.

(iv) **Developing relevant social skills:** In order to overcome loneliness one needs to develop relevant social skills. Some important skills they need to develop include the following:

- Conversational skills.
- Assertive skills.
- Overcoming shyness.
- Expressing oneself non-verbally, etc.

One way in which one can learn social skills is by approaching a good counselor who can impart relevant social skills training. In such type of training individual is exposed to models, shown video films, made to do some practical exercises, etc. They also learn to put the newly learned skill in to practice in their daily life under the guidance of a counselor or therapist.

Besides social skills training lonely individuals are also subjected to cognitive therapy to help them deal with their irrational ideas, thoughts and beliefs. Cognitive therapy teaches an individual to change their negative views of themselves and other people. Cognitive therapy teaches them to be rational and practical and evaluate their thoughts scientifically and not morally.

Questions

1. Discuss the various factors that influence our first impressions about others.
2. Write short notes on "Keeping Friends".
3. Define Loneliness and Discuss coping and overcoming Loneliness.

****

5 At Work and Play

CHOOSING CAREER

Choosing one's career is not an easy task. Career can be defined as one's purposeful life pattern of work, as seen in the sequence of jobs held throughout one's life. In order to choose a career or decide on a particular career path, we need to take a stock of our self.

Taking Stock of your Self: We need to take a stock of our self while choosing a particular career path. This requires an assessment of one's skills, interests, abilities, personality and personal values.

(i) Skills and Interests: A skill can be defined as the ability to perform a task well. It is usually developed over time through training or experience. A skill can be used to do work in many jobs or it can be used in learning. There are many different types of skills some of which are as follows:

(a) Artistic skills

(b) Communication skills

(c) Interpersonal skills

(d) Managerial skills

(e) Mechanical skills and

(f) Science skills

Besides the skill one must also have interest.

(ii) Interest: Our interest influences many aspects of our life. It influences our educational and vocational adjustment, interpersonal relationship, recreational values, etc. It was around 1920s that interest inventories first started developing as a result of the stimulation provided by the educational and vocational counselling.

Almost all the interest inventories we come across today are self-report inventories, designed to assess an individual's interest in different fields or areas of work.

Some of the important interest inventories are as follows:

1. Strong Cambell Interest Inventory.
2. Jackson Vocational Interest Survey.
3. Carccr Assessment Inventory.
4. Kuder Preference Record.
5. Holland's Self-Directed Research.
6. Thurstone Interest Schedule.
7. Sodhi and Bhatnagar Interest Inventory.
8. Interest Record by Ragu Raj Pal Singh.
9. Chatterji's Non-Language Preference Record.

Different people have different interests. Some are interested in books, others are interest in sports. These differences are also due to personal experiences and due to environment. Interest does not have a genetic base. Two important point related to interest are as follows:

- Interests change in quality and quantity along with age. The interests of a child are different from the interests of an adult.
- Environment has greater influence on interests than on abilities and aptitudes.

(iii) Abilities: Ability is what a person can do now and what he can learn to do in the future. Ability represents broad and stable characteristics responsible for a person's maximum performance on mental and physical tasks.

Ability refers to an individual's capacity to perform the various tasks in a job. It includes both what a person can do now and what he can learn to do in the future.

Abilities can be divided into two broad groups: Intellectual abilities and Physical Abilities

Intellectual Abilities: These abilities are needed to perform mental activities. Some of the important dimensions making up intellectual abilities include number aptitude, verbal comprehension, perceptual speed and inductive reasoning.

Physical abilities: These abilities are manifest in one's stamina manual dexterity, leg strength and the like. Physical abilities are required for successfully doing less-skilled and more standardised jobs. Some important physical abilities identified by psychologists are as follows.

The following table briefly summarizes the two types of abilities.

Intellectual Abilities	Physical Abilities
(1) Number Aptitude	(1) Dynamic Strength
(2) Verbal Comprehension	(2) Trunk Strength
(3) Perceptual Speed	(3) Static Strength
(4) Inductive Reasoning	(4) Explosive Strength
(5) Deductive Reasoning	(5) Extent Flexibility
(6) Spatial Visualisation	(6) Dynamic Flexibility
(7) Memory	(7) Body Coordination
(8) Word Fluency	(8) Balance
	(9) Stamina

(iv) Personality: Personality is one of the most important topics in management and behavioural sciences. There is a separate field of psychology called Personality Psychology, which is gaining great popularity among academicians, researchers and students of behavioural and management sciences.

The word personality has been derived from the Latin word "persona", which was used for the "mask" utilised by actors to change their appearances. But in Roman times it was taken as a particular character by itself. Since then, the word, personality, is used to refer not only to one's character itself but also to those aspects of individual's behaviour that set him apart from other individuals.

Leading personality theorists like Cattell, Eysenck, Allport, Walter Mischel, etc., have defined personality according to their theoretical viewpoints.

According to Lahey (1998): "Personality can be defined as the sum total of all the ways of acting, thinking, and feeling that are typical for that person and makes that person different from all other individuals."

According to Cattell: "Personality is that which permits a prediction of what a person will do in a given situation."

According to Eysenck: "Personality is more or less stable and enduring organisation of a person's character, temperament, intellect and physique, which determines his unique adjustment to the environment."

One's personality plays an important role in human adjustment and health. According, to Robbins (1998) some major personality attributes influencing human behaviour include Locus of Control, Machiavellianism, Self-esteem, Self-efficacy Type A behaviour, optimism, empathy, etc.

One's personality also plays an important role in the choice of your career.

(v) Values: Value is one of the most important and central concepts of human life. Values are those desirable states of affairs that are used as a means of justifying behaviour. Values are learned preferences. They are influenced to a considerable extent by one's upbringing and the culture to which we belong.

All values have two aspects:

(a) What is right or wrong?

(b) Rules regulating our behaviour in day-to-day situations.

The first aspect of the value deals with moral value and the second aspect of the value deals with social value.

Human beings need to be treated in a dignified manner and their individuality and personal values need to be respected. An individual's dignity and morality should always be given top priority. Even opponents and rivals should be treated with human dignity.

The values that we hold play an important role in shaping our personality. They help us to adjust better to one's own self as well as to others around them. Conflict of values create interpersonal difficulties and drains our energy.

Identifying Compatible Career: Which career is compatible for you? This is one of the most difficult questions that need to be solved with the help of an expert guide or a counselor.

(i) One of the most important sources for identifying compatible career is ***Occupational Outlook Handbook (OOH)*** published by Bureau of Labor Statistics. The handbook contains more than 20 basic career groups, each with dozens of related occupations.

An occupation is the activities and responsibilities necessary to perform given work tasks in a particular line of work such as nursing or marketing. For each career, the handbook provides information on the type of work involved, places of employment, entrance requirements, working conditions and employment outlook. The OOH also has an introductory section with helpful information on such topics as how to find a job and employment opportunities. The OOH, revised every 2 years, is available in most libraries, as well as online, www.bls.gov

(ii) Besides OOH compatible areas can also be identified by talking to teacher, school counselor, mentor or someone in your field of interest. Similarly, professors in university counseling centers and career development centers will also help you in career planning.

(iii) Compatible Careers can also be identified by taking psychological inventories consisting of psychological tests, personality tests, interests and values inventories, etc.

One of the most important interest inventories is the **Strong Interest Inventory.** This is one of the oldest, most reliable and frequently used interest inventory. It is administered by a professional counselor and is widely used for career guidance. In this inventory you can indicate your preferences for various careers, school subjects, activities, amusement, types of people, etc. There are six basic categories on the basis of which result can be scored. These are as follows:

(a) Realistic: Practical, stable, persistent, (e.g., engineer).

(b) Investigative: Task oriented, introspective and independent (e.g. biologist).

(c) Artistic: Creative, impulsive and expressive (e.g., musician).

(d) Social: Sociable, responsible and humanistic (e.g., social worker).

(e) Enterprising: Aggressive, confident and energetic (e.g., stock broker).

(f) Conventional: Predictable, conforming, conscientious and obedient (e.g., Accountant).

Scores on Strong Interest Inventory can also be scored on the following criteria:

- General career theories.
- Basic interests.
- Specific career with which you are most compatible.

Besides the scores and profile of interest inventory an assessment of an individual's abilities and personal motivation is also provided. Interest inventories are best used as an aid in making informal career choice.

Results of large number of researcher studies have revealed that Strong Interest Inventory is quite useful in predicting which people will remain in a given field.

Arriving at your Career Decisions: Arriving at a career decision involves deciding as to which is the best career for an individual. Taking decision about one's career is not only an emotional experience but it also often leads to confusion as people around you give contradictory and conflicting advice/suggestions/ opinions.

Pitfalls in Career Choice: In making a career choice one must guard against certain pitfalls which are as follows:

(a) *Accidental choice or choosing a career out of attraction:* Many individuals choose career because of attraction, glamour or external considerations. This can create problems for an individual in the future.

(b) Some of the external considerations that can influence an individual's career choice is money, prestige, power or security.

(c) Many individuals make a mistake by not exploring your career options sufficiently.

(d) Some individuals are also not particular about the time frame of their decision. They take the decision either too prematurely or take a long time to decide. For e.g., people who make career commitments in their 20's, before they are fully informed about careers often regret their choices later. Similarly, those who delay making a career commitment until their 30's usually deprive themselves of the necessary work experience to make a wise choice.

(e) One more common error that people make is they rigidly stick to the career initially chosen and are not flexible enough to modify their initial choice.

Preparing for your Career: Once a career choice has been made, individuals must prepare for it so that he/she successfully achieves the career goals. One enters career in several ways.

- Through apprenticeship training.
- Training through vocational technical school.
- Internship.
- On-the-job training program.
- After completing a college degree (3-5 years).

Few careers such as doctors, lawyers, chartered accountants, etc., require registration with their professional bodies. In some countries license is required from State (Government) to practice a given profession. Thus, professions such as Clinical Psychology, Law, Medicines require:

- Advance degree
- Supervised training
- State license

Career planning also requires fulfilling appropriate educational requirements for a chosen career. Preparing for a career requires the following:

(a) Appropriate educational qualification
(b) Preparing a resume
(c) Facing an interview
(d) Searching appropriate places for jobs, as more than 80 % of the jobs are never advertised. One can search jobs at following places:
    - Apply in person or walk in the door with your resume.
    - Search internet job sites such as monster.com, naukri.com, etc.
    - Enroll in employment agency.
    - Take help of management consultants or recruiting firms.
    - Use the services of University/College Career Center.
    - Use parent's personal contacts or network.
    - Newspaper, Professional Journals, etc.
    - Visiting jobs fairs, etc.

One of the most important strategies is networking i.e., using personal contacts to establish career opportunities.

CAREER OUTLOOK

How does one look at one's career. Today, there is a lot of dynamism or change in a given career. Do you know the outlook of your chosen career? Are the jobs openings in your field expected to remain stable? Two important topics related to career outlook worth discussing are as follows:

- Forecasting your career's growth
- Changing jobs/careers

We would discuss each of these briefly

Forecasting your Career's Growth: Changes in economy, technological developments, political conditions, etc., considerably influence jobs that will be available in the future. Today, the service sectors, such as finance, real estate, health care, communication, data processing, etc., are expected to dominate employment. Jobs in these areas would be readily available in future. In contrast manufacturing, goods producing, services and administrative support positions are expected to grow at a much slower rate.

Changing Jobs or Career: One must remember that it is perfectly natural to modify one's career goal. People are often reluctant to change their career goals due to many reasons, some of which are as follows:

(i) They do not want to disappoint parents, spouses or peers.

(ii) People also fear that switching career goals may be regarded as an admission of failure.

(iii) They often underestimate their new career goal.

(iv) They do not want to face difficulties, insecurity surrounding new jobs or want to go through the adjustment process which will require effort (physical as well as mental) for switching from one career to another.

At present people are more frequently changing their jobs than in the past? Today, an individual tends to hold several brief jobs in the first few years after graduation, and then settles into a position that lasts several years.

Individuals change jobs/career due to many reasons. One of the most common reasons is Burnout, which can be defined as a psychological syndrome of emotional exhaustion, depersonalization and reduced personal accomplishment that occurs among individuals, especially those who do "people work".

CONTEMPORARY ISSUES IN THE WORLD OF WORK

There are many issues in the world of work that needs consideration, a few of which are as follows:

1. Job Satisfaction
2. Technology and Work
3. Diversity in the Workplace

We would discuss each of these briefly.

1. Job Satisfaction: It can be defined as people's feelings about different aspects of their jobs, how well one likes a given job, depending on such factors as pay, co-worker, etc. Job satisfaction is influenced by wide variety of factors.

(i) Work activity
(ii) Working conditions on the job
(iii) Age
(iv) Sex
(v) Years on jobs

Some important points with respect to job satisfaction worth considering are as follows:

- People generally prefer work that involves (a) contact with others (b) is interesting (c) offers the opportunity to learn new skills and (d) allows them independence.
- There is a moderate positive correlation between performance and job satisfaction.
- Working conditions influence job satisfaction.

Some important conditions that influence job satisfaction include:

- Opportunities for advancement.
- Job security.
- Good working hours.
- Friendly, cooperative co-workers.
- Considerate supervisors.
- Work that allows some control over decision making is perceived to be more satisfying.
- Highest paying jobs does not necessarily increase one's job satisfaction.
- Recent graduates (new entrants) are generally satisfied

with their jobs as compared to person who have put few years on the jobs. As soon as the novelty wears off and reality sets in job satisfaction reduces sharply. After 5 years on the job, satisfaction tends to rise steadily with age and years on the job. This is generally due to three reasons:- a) Greater job security, b) Better pay and c) Realistic expectations.

2. Technology and Work: Introduction of new technology such as computers, telecommunications, videoconferencing, etc., is influencing as to how we work. Many employees use technology for their personal work or may misuse technology at work. For e.g., an employee may view pornography during lunch time or would use emails for personal work rather than office work. Psychologist has used the term cyber slacking to refer to the over use of the internet in the workplace for purposes other then work. Some common problems and ethical issues raised due to technology at workplace include:

- Cyber harassment
- Chain emails
- Joke emails
- Objectionable forms of communication through email

Technology has considerably changed our working life. One such change is e-recruiting, in which job candidates are screened by phone, video or computer rather than in a face-to-face interview.

3. Diversity in the Workplace: Diversity in the workplace is increasing with the reduction of regional and national barriers and as a result of globalization of work. Increased diversity has brought many problems that require new adjustments and skills.

Employees will have to learn cultural similarities and differences and understand cross cultural differences that exist between groups. Employees will have to acquire knowledge about other's culture. Those individuals who come from individualistic cultures (such as USA, Europe) have different personality characteristics as compared to those coming from collectivist cultures.

More and more women are entering work force and their distribution in work force is uneven. Women are over presented in careers such as teaching, secretaries, nurses, librarians but they are underrepresented in careers such as engineers, dentists and physicians. Working women face many issues, chief among them include:

- Role conflict between work and home
- Opportunities for advancement
- Sexual harassment
- Problems of child care, etc.
- Glass ceiling

Balancing family and work responsibilities is a major problem faced by people at workplace.

LEISURE TIME

Leisure can be defined as time free from work or duty that may be spent in recreational activities of one's choice. The purpose of leisure according to Aristotle is cultivation of the self and the pursuit of the higher things of life. It should be remembered that maintenance activities are not leisure. Maintenance activities include non-leisure and non-work time spent in activities necessary for the maintenance of life.

One type of leisure is unconditional leisure. It refers to activities which are chosen, excluding work and maintenance activities.

Work and Leisure: Individuals must learn to balance work and leisure. Most people regard work and leisure as non-overlapping and separate aspects of their work life. One's leisure activities are considerably influenced by factors such as

- Age
- Sex
- Race/religion
- Socio-cultural and educational level

Using Leisure Positively: Positive use of leisure requires certain degree of choice and planning. One type of leisure that is most common among Americans is taking a vacation? Leisure is most important during midlife years. Constructive leisure activities are an important way to prepare for retirement. People who have developed rewarding leisure activities as well as a network of social and family relationships are more able to make the crucial shift from full time to satisfying retirement. One common and very constructive leisure activity is volunteer work.

Questions

1. Write short notes on the following:
   (a) Identifying Compatible Careers
   (b) Arriving at Career Decisions
2. Write a note on Career Outlook.
3. Discuss the various contemporary issues in the World of Work.

   Or

   Write short notes on the following:
   1. Job Satisfaction
   2. Technology and Work
   3. Diversity in the Workplace
4. Write a note on Leisure Time.

****

6 Sexuality, Love and Commitment

SEXUALITY: MEN AND WOMEN; SEXUAL RESPONSIVENESS; PRACTICAL ISSUES

Sexuality is an important subject related to human adjustment as well as interpersonal attraction. It involves important issues and concerns which we will discuss in this section.

Men and Women

Men and women differ with respect to sexuality. Three important sub-topics within this section are as follows;

- Changing views on Sexuality
- Sexual Communication
- Initiating and Refusing Sex

We would discus each of these briefly

1. Changing Views on Sexuality: Men and women often misunderstand each other sexually. Most of the misunderstanding is due to gender stereotypes, which can be defined as widespread generalities about the characteristics and behavior of men and women that exaggerates the differences between the sexes, thereby setting the stage for misunderstanding and frustration.

A common stereotype belief is that:-

- Men have a stronger sex drive than women.
- Men enjoy sex more than women do.

It has also been found that:-

- Women fantasize about having sex with familiar partner, while men often fantasize about sex with strangers.

- Men's attitude, with regard to sex is more permissive and promiscuous as compared to women.

Differences between men and women have evolutionary heritage and has helped each sex adapt better to situation and multiply their genetic material.

Men are inherently sexually assertive with some men downright aggressive. On the other hand women are perceived to be less sexually aggressive and assertive. The aggressive dimension of sex in men may take the form of 'power', 'experience' and 'domination'. A similar dimension did not exist for women.

Two other differences between Men and Women which are worth noting with respect to sexuality are as follows:

- Certain behavior such as initiating sex or expressing affection is thought to be natural prerogative of men. On the other hand women (more than men) tend to "romanticize" or feel that love ought to play an important role in sexuality.
- Women are also likely to endorse sexuality in a committed relationship whereas men are more likely to engage in casual sex.

Recent research has revealed that only few people are 100 % masculine or feminine. In recent years women have become more masculine and men have become more androgynous. The term androgyny refers to the combination of desirable masculine and feminine characteristic in one person. The opposite of androgyny is sex–typed.

Research studies have demonstrated that androgyny is a preferred sex-role orientation and can help an individual adapt and adjust better in different situations.

Changes in gender role and sexuality are giving rise to a healthier view of sexuality. Some new ideas in the area of sexuality are as follows:

- Sex is not something a man *does to* or *for a* woman or vice versa. Sex is something that a man and a woman *do together* as equal participants.
- Women have become more assertive with regards to her performance in the area of sexuality.
- Partners have come to realize that sexual urges vary with

mood, time and place.

- Sexual pleasure is often correlated with partner's response. If one partner is critical, unresponsive or at best passive, the emotional vitality of the couple's sex life weakens and eventually, withers away.
- When both partners are actively involved and when each person spontaneously communicates feelings, the other person's excitement and responsiveness is heightened (i.e., increased).
- Quality of overall relationship influences sexual relationship.

2. Sexual Communication: How often do people share communication about sexuality with others, especially their partners. It is not easy for people to express their sexual desires or preferences. How easily can you communicate with your partner your sexual wants or desires?

- One of the most reluctant areas to talk is that of sexuality. Most people are reluctant to talk about sex with their lovers or spouses. It is as if talking about sex would spoil their spontaneity. It is important to note that couples should avoid talking about sex immediately before or after, because one's partner may become defensive or sensitive to a given comment or suggestion from another partner and this can create conflict between couples.
- It is also best to avoid discussing about sex in a calculating or clinical way.
- Partner's sexual preferences, likes and dislikes should be probed gradually and over a period of time rather in a few sittings at length.
- Communication with respect to sex matters is most successful when it is a two way communication with both partners expressing themselves and discussing freely on a given topic/issue. Many individuals, both men and women, are not open in communication or do not give enough feedback to each other.
- The most important part of sexual communication is the attitude you and your partner have towards each other.
- The most crucial part is the sense of trust and mutual empathy — the sense that each cares for other and knows this feeling is reciprocated.

Sexual communication can take many forms as follows:

(a) Making a direct request for e.g., "I would prefer doing something together before we have sex such as taking a walk on a beach "or "I prefer you wearing a pink dress", etc.

(b) Using questions to discover your partner's preferences. You can ask either a "YES" or "NO" question such as " Did you like it" or you can ask any open ended questions such as "what part of our sexuality would you most like to improve?" You can also ask an either......or question such as "do you want to talk about this now or at a later time?" It has been noted that open-ended and either or questions encourage more participation from partners than simple yes-or-no questions.

Questions should be most selectively used and must not be asked in ways to create doubt or damage the self-esteem of the partner. One of the most sensitive areas related to sexual communication is concerning giving and receiving criticism regarding sexuality. Some highly destructive patterns have been identified.

Destructive Patterns of Communication: The most common destructive patterns are as follows:

(a) One pattern is **criticism** that involves attacking partner's character for e.g., calling the partner "selfish".

(b) Second pattern is **contempt** in which insults are used to denigrate the partner's sexuality.

(c) Third damaging communicating pattern is **defensiveness** in which an individual make excuses or uses some other self-protective defense.

(d) **Withdrawal:** In this form of communication a person withdraws from sexual communication. In this form of communication person ignores the partner either by watching TV or turning one's back on them. Withdrawal is very much lethal (damaging) to sexual relationship.

Some important points related to criticism which are worth nothing are as follows:

- Offer criticisms only when there is a good reason, otherwise avoid it.
- Offer criticism at an appropriate time and place.
- Express your remarks in non-judgmental ways, generally using 'I' messages.

- If your partner has criticized do not overreact.
- Criticism should be viewed as a concern and care from the partner's side rather than an attack on oneself.
- Be careful of your non-verbal communication. It should indicate interest, openness and concern rather than display of negative feelings and behavior.

3.Initiating and Refusing Sex: How does one initiate sex or refuse sex. Very often initiation is not verbal. We generally do not say "let us have sex", "can we have sex". Instead we indulge in actions or indirect talks, which take you towards initiation of sex or refusal of sex.

Traditionally men take lead in initiating sex. Many women too prefer that men take lead. Today, the scene is changing. Women are also becoming active in not only initiating sex but also refusing it. Women who were active in initiating or refusing sex were found to be more satisfied in their sex life as compared to who were not so active.

Initiating and refusing sex not only means actual sexual acts but also related things such as sexual communication, talking about sexual matters concerning oneself such as "examination of breasts", "experience of watching a sexual film", etc., and asking about one's sexual history i.e., "When did you had sex last", "Can you tell about your sexual experiences in past", etc. It has been found that those who share sexual histories with their partners have the following characteristics:

- They use contraception more frequently.
- They are less likely to use drug and alcohol.
- They believe more in committed relationship.

SEXUAL RESPONSIVENESS

William Masters and Virginia Johnson have done considerable research on sexual responsiveness. They found that individuals respond to sex in terms of a cycle which they called it as "the sexual response cycle", which we will discuss:

The Sexual Response Cycle: Masters and Johnson through a series of studies using interviews and controlled observation of volunteers found that human sexual response consists of five stages as follows:

1. Transition (or desire)
2. Excitement
3. Plateau
4. Orgasm
5. Resolution

We would discuss each of these stages briefly:

1. Transition (or Desire): This stage can be defined as a gradual shift from a non-sexual to a sexual state of being and includes the awakening of sexual desire and a readiness for sexual arousal. Transition stage makes an individual "get ready" for sex. Individuals differ widely with regards to what puts them in a mood for sex. Something that can only facilitate the transition include the following:

- Relaxation
- Candle-lit meal
- Dancing
- Listening to certain music
- Watching a romantic or erotic movies
- Touching
- Massages
- Relaxing in hot water
- Walking on a beach, etc

Lack of sexual desire generally stems from partner's un-readiness for sex. Men are generally more impatient and less in tune for transition than women. In general women prefer a more gradual transition, accompanied by emotional sharing and tender caressing and kissing. Some individuals use erotic, material, images, sounds, etc., to stimulate or "turn on" their partners.

2. Excitement: The term excitement is roughly equivalent to sexual arousal. Three important changes that occur as a result of excitement are as follows:

- Increased muscle tension
- Engorgement of the genitals with blood
- Increased heart rate

Sexual arousal is heightened through stimulation of the senses. Stimulating the erogenous zones almost always intensifies sexual arousal. It is during this stage that man's penis becomes erect and the women experiences arousal of her sex organs. The length of this stage varies greatly among individual from few minutes to hours or so.

Sexual arousal also depends on psychological changes in CNS, such as thoughts and feelings about specific partner or the sexual act.

Different things may stimulate men and women. The most common factor that may lead to sexual arousal is exposure to "erotic fantasies". For some people erotic fantasy provides an initial boost to sexual arousal. Erotic fantasy is usually created or recalled from memory. Sexual fantasies have useful purpose:

- They reduce anxiety.
- They help to focus on thoughts and feelings and thus help to avoid distractions.
- Sexual fantasies help to counteract boredom, especially in a long-term relationship.

There are gender differences in fantasies.

(a) Men fantasize about women's bodies, physical appearance and sexual activity.

(b) Women fantasize about their own attractiveness to men.

(c) Women fantasize about the emotional or romantic context of the sexual activity.

3. Plateau: It is a stage prior to orgasm where sexual arousal becomes pronounced. There is a brief stage lasting from few seconds to several minutes. During this stage usual signs of sexual arousal become more pronounced such as

- Erection of man's penis.
- Lubrication of the women's vagina.
- The heart beats faster.
- Breathing grows more rapid.
- Increasing muscle tension and blood pressure lead to engorgement of the sex organs.
- Women experience a marked increase in the swelling of the outer third of the vaginal, making stimulation even more pleasurable.

During this phase a particular partner (generally men) will have to slow down so that he dose not reach orgasm quickly. Partners generally prefer delaying reaching orgasm so that they can continue with the pleasure of sexual arousal and plateau phase for a longer time.

4. Orgasm: It is the climax of sexual excitement that is pleasurable and releases tension. Men generally reach orgasm first as compared to women. During the stage of orgasm muscles in and around the man's penis contract rhythmically, causing the forcible ejaculation of semen. Similarly, the outer third of the women's vagina contracts rhythmically along with pulsation of her uterus. For both sexes, the first few contractions are the most intense and pleasurable, followed by weaker and slower contractions.

5. Resolution: It is a stage in which the body, after orgasm, returns to its normal, non-excited phase. Some important changes that occur during resolution phase are as follows:

- Heart rate, breathing, blood pressure. etc., quickly subsides.
- Muscle tension usually dissipates within 05 minutes after orgasm.
- Men loose about 50 percent of their erection within a minute or so after orgasm and the remainder in the next several minutes.
- Men enter into a ***refractory period*** - a time when added stimulation will not result in orgasm. The refractory period varies form few hours to days in men. As people age refractory period is influenced by many factors such as:
  (a) Age
  (b) Health
  (c) Frequency of previous sexual activity
  (d) Sexual desire

Women generally have no refractory period or very short refractory period. Most women are physically, capable of another orgasm, though they may not desire it or experience it.

Individual Differences: There are individual differences in matters of sexuality between different sexes:

1. For e.g., men and women differ considerably with respect to refractory period.
2. Men and women also differ with respect to sexual arousal. Brain imaging studies have revealed that when exposed to sexually arousing material, male amygdala and hypothalamus are more strongly activated in men as compared to women.

3. Cultural factors play a stronger role in restricting women's sexuality as compared to men. Certain cultures are tolerant of certain sexual conducts in men but not in case of women.
4. Women are more likely than men to report being affected by:
   - Fear of pregnancy
   - Guilt
   - Lack of desire
   - Social disapproval
5. Differences between male and female sexuality tend to change across one's life span:
   - Teenage male sexuality is very intense and almost exclusively genitally focused.
   - In case of women, sexual awakening occurs later in teens and late 20s, their arousal and orgasmic response is slow and inconsistent. By 30s women's sexual responsivity becomes more quicker and intense, especially among experienced women.
   - Adolescent male sexuality is body centered and the person centered aspects are incorporated later. Adolescent female sexuality is more people centered and the body centered aspects of sex tend to be added later in women's development.
   - Men seem to begin with an intense, genetically focused sexuality and only later develop an appreciation for the sensuous and emotional aspects of sex. In contrast, women have an earlier awareness of the sensuous and emotional aspect of sex and tend to develop the capacity for intense genital response later.
   - Men and women also differ greatly with respect to orgasmic experience. Men generally experience single orgasm in a sexual act, a women can have multiple orgasms. Women are more likely to have multiple orgasms - two or more sexual climaxes within a short period of time. Multiple orgasms is an exception in case of men.
   - Men and women also differ with respect to preference for sex partners.

While studying individual differences with respect to sexuality it is also important to understand the concept of sexual orientation and its different aspects and dimensions.

Sexual Orientation: It is defined as a component of sexuality that is characterized by enduring emotional, romantic or sexual attraction to a particular gender. The three major types of sexual orientation are as follows:

(a) **Homosexuality**- emotional and sexual preference for partners of the same sex. Homosexual men are often called as gays and women as lesbians.

(b) **Heterosexuality**- emotional and sexual preference for partners of the opposite sex.

(c) **Bisexuality**- It means that individuals prefers sex with partners of either sex.

Some heterosexual individuals are ***Homophobic***, a term used to refer to fear of homosexual or negative attitudes that one holds towards homosexuals. According to some researchers instead of the term homophobia we should use the term sexual prejudice. Homosexual individuals face considerable stigma in society, especially in India. They are also psychologically vulnerable to suicidal ideation, suicide attempt, self-injurious behavior, etc. Homosexuality is not considered a form of mental disorder but the stigma attached to it can contribute to depression and other mental disorders.

Love and Sex: The relationship between love and sex has been considerably explored by the scholars but understood little by individuals. The relationship between love and sex creates considerable adaptation problems among many individuals. Three important points which are worth noting with respect to love and sex are as follows:

- Love and sex need not go together. An individual can derive pleasure from sex without being in love.
- Masters and Johnson observed that there is nothing inherently "bad" about sex, without love, especially if both partners consent.
- Under certain circumstances for some people sex without love may be enjoyable in its own right. However, in reality, great deal depends on individual's value system. Many individuals strongly believe that there is an intimate relationship between love and sex and that sex without love is only a lust. Psychologists believe that love can enrich sex especially in long-term relationship, like marriage.

Couples who indulge in sex mechanically, especially when one or both partners have little or no affection for the other sex, is no longer satisfying.

The relationship between love and sex can also vary with respect to types of love. There are three different types of love.

(a) **Romantic Love:** It consists of intimacy (or closeness) and passion. It leads to satisfying sex at least for a while.

(b) **Companionate Love:** It is a kind of loving but practical relationship based primarily on emotional closeness and commitment rather than physical, sexual intimacy. The sex life of individuals who are in companionate love can be highly disappointing in some cases.

(c) **Consummate Love:** It is defined as a complete and balanced love characterized by emotional closeness sexual intimacy of commitment between the partners.

PRACTICAL ISSUES

There are many practical issues concerning sexuality that requires our adjustment and adaptation. Some important practical issues related to sexuality are as follow:

1. Sexual Dysfunction
2. Contraception
3. Sexually Transmitted Diseases
4. Sexual Victimization

We would discuss each of these briefly:

1. Sexual Dysfunction: It can be defined as persistent problems that prevent an individual from engaging in or enjoying sexual intercourse. Sexual dysfunction can be grouped in various ways:-

One classification of sexual dysfunction is on the basis of the phase of the sexual response cycle. These include:-difficulties of desire, arousal and orgasm.

(a) Hypoactive Sexual Desire [Inhibited Sexual Desire]: It refers to lack of interest in sex. Women suffer more from this problem. Inhibited sexual desire can occur under following conditions:

- When there is a family problem or problems at work.
- Boredom

- Anger
- Psychological factors such as anxiety, guilt, low self-esteem, depression, etc., can lower one's sex desire.

(b) Aversion to Sex: It includes anxiety, disgust, repulsion and other negative emotions towards sex. Sexual aversions are very common among women as compared to men. Aversion to sex can occur under following conditions:-

- If one is a victim of repeated sex abuse, incest, etc.
- When one is forced into sex through pressure or bargaining.
- Repeated unsuccessful attempts to please a sexual partner may lead to avoidance of sex.
- Anxiety about conflicts in one's sexual identity or orientation may create fear for sex.

(c) Inhibited Sexual Arousal: This dysfunction can occur in men as well women and it can take many forms:

(i) Primary Erectile Inhibition (Impotency).

(ii) Inhibited Vaginal Lubrications (when insufficient vaso-congestion and insufficient lubrication occur in women). Normally during sexual stimulation, the congestion of blood vessels causes the vaginal walls to secrete droplets of fluid which eventually form a shiny film on the walls of the vagina. Lack of lubrication is one cause of inhibited sexual arousal or pain during sexual intercourse.

(iii) Secondary Erectile Inhibition: It occurs in men. It is diagnosed in conditions when men have previously experienced erections but are consistently unable to have an erection of sufficient firmness to penetrate women's vagina. Erectile inhibition may be due to many factors:-

- Psychological/emotional factors.
- Physiological factors such as diabetes, effects of certain drugs such as alcohol, narcotics, amphetamines, etc.
- Reaction to certain medications.
- Worry and criticism from a partner also lead to erectile dysfunction.
- It also occurs when an individual performs a "spectator's role" i.e., instead of relaxing and letting his erection occur spontaneously, he watches and judges his own performance. Self critical attitude on one's part also contributes to erectile dysfunction.

(d) Premature or Retarded Ejaculation (In Women it is called as Female Orgasmic Disorder):- In premature ejaculation there is early orgasm in a man, as a result, man's enjoyment of sex is significantly lessened or his partner is not contented.

Doing sex in a "hurry" can also be one of the causes of premature ejaculation. In the case of women there is considerable variability. There are few women who have never experienced orgasm. There are others who need direct clitoral stimulation either manual, oral, or, through self stimulation.

2. Contraception: Contraception means *"Prevention of conception or impregnation"*. Contraception is the use of various devices, drugs, agents, sexual practices, or surgical procedures to prevent conception or impregnation (pregnancy). Contraception helps women plan if and when they want to have a baby. The condom is the only current contraception device that helps protect sexual partners from STIs (sexually transmitted infections).

Contraception was earlier used to control the birth of a child but today as a result of spread of AIDS contraception has received renewed attention as a means to prevent sexually transmitted diseases. Today, many reliable contraceptives are available. However, knowledge about it and inhibitions associated with it, has come in the way of effective use of contraception.

Barriers to Effective Contraception: Effective contraception requires that couples should negotiate as to when to use contraception, who will use it and what type of contraception will be used. Following steps are involved in determining the effective use of contraception.

(i) Determining how often one would be sexually active.

(ii) Couples would have to acquire knowledge about fertility and conception.

(iii) The contraception that they would decide to use must be readily available.

(iv) They must also have the motivation and skill to use the method.

(v) Failure to skip any one of these steps would result in pregnancy.

Use of contraception is a shared responsibility and both the partners should discuss it jointly as to who will use contraception and when.

3. Sexual Transmitted Diseases (also once called as Venereal Diseases): It refers to a group of disorder that may be transmitted primarily through sexual interaction. Some of the most common sexually transmitted diseases that we would discuss briefly are as follows:-

(i) Chlamydia
(ii) Gonorrhea
(iii) Genital herpes
(iv) Syphilis
(v) AIDS

(i) Chlamydia: It is most commonly found among males as well as females. Men who contact infection have symptoms which are similar to gonorrhea which includes:

- Discharge from penis
- Mild burning sensation during urination.

Women with Chlamydia infection show little or no symptoms and are often not aware of the diseases. If left untreated in women, it may result in cervical inflammation or pelvic inflammatory diseases.

(ii) Gonorrhea: It is a common sexually transmitted bacterial infection that sometimes produces a cloudy, smelly discharge and a burning sensation upon urination. Untreated Gonorrhea in men leads to sterility. In women untreated Gonorrhea leads to inflammation of fallopian tubes, infertility, birth malformations, menstrual disorders, etc.

(iii) Genital Herpes: It is one type of herpes viral infection that is primarily transmitted through sexual contact.

(iv) Syphilis: It is caused by a spiral shaped bacterium or spirochete.

(v) AIDS: Though it is classified as a sexually transmitted diseases, it can also be contacted through blood or blood products containing the virus.

HIV does not readily penetrate intact body surfaces, so there is little danger of getting it through a kiss, a sneeze, a handshake or a toilet seat. HIV is acquired by direct exposure of one's blood stream to the virus, which is carried by body fluids – notably blood and semen.

In homosexual men, the main source of transmission has been anal intercourse.

Common Symptoms of AIDS

- Progressive, unexplained weight loss
- Persistent fever (accompanied by night sweats)
- Swollen lymph nodes in the neck, armpits, groin.
- Reddish purple spots on the skin.
- Chronic fatigue
- Unexplained diarrhea.

4. Sexual Victimization: Sexual victimization is said to have occurred when a person is coerced to engage in sexual acts under duress or force. Sexual victimization may take many forms, some of which are as follows:

- Sexual Abuse of Children
- Child Pornography
- Rape

We would discuss each of them in brief:-

(i) Sexual Abuse of Children: In case of sexual abuse of children, most often the abuser is a family member, close relative or friend. In many instances sexual abuse is not limited to single episode and may not involve physical force.

Effects of Child Sexual Abuse: The immediate effects of child sexual abuse include:

- Increased anxiety
- Anger
- Eating or sleep disturbance
- Guilt
- Withdrawal
- Psychological problems of adjustment
- Abused child may also be preoccupied with sex such as unusual interest in sex organs, sex play and nudity.
- Sex abused children also exhibit a host of physical complaints, such as rashes, headaches and vomiting which has no medical basis.

In adulthood victims of sex abuse display the following symptoms:-

- Difficulties engaging in sex
- Compulsively engaging in sex
- Abused women may feel isolated and distrustful of men. They are likely to be anxious, depressed and guilt-ridden.
- Boys who are sexually abused are at risk of becoming child molesters.

(ii) Child Pornography: It can bc dcfined as a visual depiction of a minor engaging in sexually explicit, conduct, especially one lacking serious literary, artistic, political or scientific value.

Most individual depicted in child pornography are girls between the age group of 6 and 12 years.

(iii) Rape: It is defined as the sexual intercourse under conditions of actual or threatened force that overcome the victim's resistance. One type of rape is called as ***Date Rape,*** which refers to coercive sexual activity that occurs during a date.

Rape has devastating effects on victim's mental health. Almost one third of all rape victims develop rape related Posttraumatic Stress Disorder (RR-PTDS). Sometimes, during their lives, RR-PTSD dramatically increases the victim's risk for major alcohol and drug abuse problems. Rape survivors experience variety of emotional repercussions in two phases:-

(a) Acute Phase: It begins immediately after the assault. Victim cries, gets largely disoriented, and upset, she experiences anxiety, shame, guilt, anger, self blame and sense of powerlessness. Physical symptoms include nausea, headache, pain syndrome, etc.

(b) Reorganization Phase: The second phase is called as the reorganization phase, which last for a very long time, in few cases entire life period.

Rape is a very traumatic experience which interferes more with psychological aspects of sexual activity than the physiological response.

LOVE AND INTIMACY; COMMITMENT; ADJUSTING TO INTIMATE RELATIONSHIPS

Love and Commitment

Love and Commitment are important topics dealing with human adjustment. Some of the important sub-topics of this section are briefly outlined below:

1. Love and Intimacy
2. Commitment
3. Adjusting to Intimate Relationships
4. Divorce and its Consequences

1. Love and Intimacy: Love and intimacy are important aspects of adjustment in one's personal life. The topic of love and intimacy is closely related to friendship and close-relationship. The two important sub-topics within this topic are as follows:

(A) The Ingredients of Love

(B) Love and Close Relationship.

We would discuss each of these briefly:-

A. The Ingredients of Love: Love is one of the extreme ends of positive attraction. It can be defined as a deep and tender feeling of affection for or attachment to one or more person. Love relationships include characteristics such as:-

- Fascination
- Sexual desire
- Exclusiveness
- Intense caring for each other.

It is due to the above characteristics of greater exclusiveness and emotional involvement between the lovers that they experience greater conflict, distress and mutual criticisms in their relationships than do friends.

Three Types of Love: The three major types of love are as follows:-

(i) Romantic love

(ii) Passionate love

(iii) Companionate love

Romantic love can be defined as the strong emotional attachment to a person of the opposite sex and on few occasion, the same sex.

Elaine Hatfield (1988) identified the two types of love: Passionate and Companionate .

Passionate Love is equivalent to romantic love. It is defined as an intense emotional reaction to a potential romantic partner who may not even love you in return. Three important conditions must be met in order for individuals to feel that they have fallen madly in love.

- Individual must be exposed to romantic images (as in the media) and role models that lead to expectation that love is possible.
- Individual must come into contact with an "appropriate" person to love.
- Intense arousal must be present which is interpreted as love.

Companionate love can be defined as loving but practical relationship based primarily on emotional closeness and commitment rather than physical, sexual intimacy. Companionate love is a practical love that involves trust, caring and tolerance for the partner's faith.

Companionate love is more moderately emotional than passionate love. Companionate love, as compared to passionate love, takes longer to develop. Companionate love tends to be more characteristics of long-term relationships, including happy marriages and some friendships.

Triangular Theory of Love: Robert Sternberg and Susan Grajek (2004) developed the triangular theory of love. According to them love has following three components:

(i) Intimacy
(ii) Passion
(iii) Commitment

Intimacy: It is the emotional aspect of love and includes closeness, sharing, communication and support. Intimacy tends to develop slowly in the beginning and then progress more steadily until it levels off and later declines. An apparent lack of intimacy may mean that the relationship is dying.

Passion: It is the emotional or motivational aspect of love, involves physiological arousal and an intense desire to be united with the loved one.

Commitment: It is the cognitive aspects of love, includes both short term affirmation of your love for the person and the long term commitment to maintain that love. Commitment usually develops in a more straight forward manner than does intimacy or passion. In long lasting relationships, commitment increases gradually at first and then more rapidly.

As the relationship continues the amount of commitment levels off. If the relationship begins to weaken the level of commitment will decline. If the relationship falls apart, commitment falls back to zero.

Some important points with respect to love which are worth noting are as follows:

- Love has been found to be an important basis for establishing a marriage especially in Individualistic Societies such as USA. An Individualistic Society is one where the goals of individual are more important than the goals of the Collective (or of the Society).
- Those individuals who assigned greater importance to love came from countries with higher economic standards than those who did not do so.
- Passionate love has been found to be highly correlated with mental satisfaction, i.e., the higher the passion, the higher the mental satisfaction.

The following figure depicts the Triangular Theory of Love.

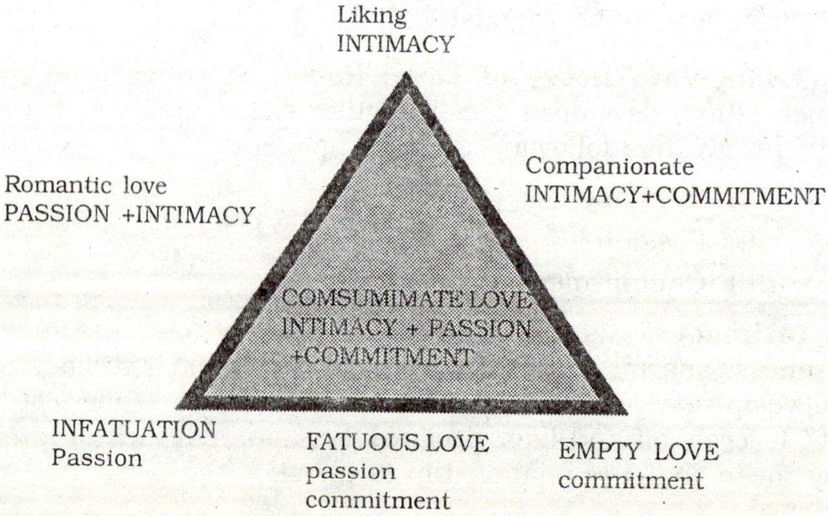

Love and Close Relationship: Love and close relationship has also been found to be considerably influenced by one's attachment style.

Attachment Style: It means our typical style of becoming involved with others. Hazen and Phillips Shaver (1994) have done considerable research in this area. They identified three different types of attachment styles as follows:-

(a) Securely Attached

(b) Avoidant Attachment

(c) Anxious Ambivalent

We would discuss each of these briefly:

(a) Securely Attached: Securely attached people believe that it is easy to get close to others and they report happy and trusting love relationships. Their romances last the longest. These individuals feel that romantic love never fades. Securely attached individuals come from families in which their parents were warm, loving and responsive.

(b) Avoidant Attachments: These individuals feel uneasy when people get too close to them. These individuals:

- Fear intimacy.
- Have trouble trusting and depending on others.
- Are prone to jealousy.
- Hold a cynical picture of love, believing that the head-over-heels romantic love depicted in movies and novels does not exits in real life.
- Believe that romantic love seldom lasts.
- Believe that it is rare to find someone to fall in love with.
- Came from families, where their mothers were rejecting and father was uncaring.

(c) Anxious – Ambivalent: In this group are included those individuals who desire a high level of closeness but their partners are not willing to give. These individuals experience emotional extremes as well as jealousy in their relationships. They find it easy to "fall in love" but difficult to find "true love". Some important characteristic features of this attachment style are as follows:

- About 20% of the adults manifest this form of attachment style.

- These adults are obsessive and preoccupied with their relationship.
- These individuals are highly demanding, want more relationship closeness from their partners and experience feelings of jealousy.
- They also have fear of being abandoned by their partners.
- They generally come from families where parents displayed less warmth towards them and their parent's marriage was mostly unhappy.

Commitment: Close relationship involves commitment. It can take form of cohabitation or marriage.

1. Cohabitation: It is the practice of unmarried persons living together, including indulging in sexual relationship. Cohabitation is on the rise in many Indian cities including Mumbai. The number of Cohabitating Couples in the United States has grown six fold from the 1970s till date. One of the important consequences of cohabitation is Cohabitation Effect, where couples that cohabit first have greater marital instability then couples that do not cohabit. Cohabitation does not result in marriage, and when it does, it is more likely to result in divorce.

Research studies have revealed that about half of the cohabiting couple's eventually marry.

2. Marriage and other Committed Relationship: Marriage is one of the most committed forms of relationship. It is a universal relationship in that almost all people generally get married. Marriage is a legal union between two people and involves intimacy and close relationship. Marriage is considered to be the most essential relationship which is seen as promoting the welfare of children and stability of society. The median age of marriage has been gradually increasing at least in metros. The phenomenon of homosexual marriage has also received considerably media attention in India in recent years, though such a relationship has no legal basis.

More than 50% of the marriages are ending in divorce. Once marital success was measured in terms of longevity of marriage. However, today success in marriage is interpreted more in terms of marital relationship rather than its duration. Marital satisfaction is generally defined as the sense of gratification and contentment in marriage. Gottman (2000) found that there are certain emotions and styles that prove toxic for new marriages, these include:-

- Criticism
- Contempt
- Defensiveness and
- Withdrawal

For healthy marriage, it is also very essential that one partner should give another partner that benefits of doubt in difficult times or remain emotionally disengaged in relationship. Negative emotions especially on the part of men often cause discord in marriage.

Factors contributing to Long-Term Marital Satisfaction: What leads to satisfaction in marriage. Successful marriages have following characteristics.

(a) Joint problem solving ability: Couples who reports successful marriages have also reported that they solve problems jointly.

(b) Having fun together: Happily married couples "have fun" together and cherish such experiences. They indulge in "fun", "playfullness" and "humor".

(c) Open communication: Happily married couples have open and honest communication. They are free to discuss, communicate, share and talk to their partners. Good communication between couples increases marital satisfaction.

(d) Affective Affirmation: It is one of the strongest predictor of marital success. Affective affirmation involves the Communication of:-

- Love
- Accepting attitudes
- Unconditional approval of one's mate

(e) Other Factors: Some important factors that lead to marital satisfactions are as follows:

- Empathic ability for understanding partner's feelings.
- A good balance of time spent together and separately.
- Satisfying sexual relationship and
- Mutual willingness to make adjustments for each other.

It has also been observed that happy couples are more likely to place importance on interpersonal intimacy and commitment to a lasting relationship than on practical satisfaction.

Self-disclosure: It is one important aspect of successful marriage. Self-disclosure refers to the sharing of intimate or personal information with one another. High self-disclosure often leads to following:

- High relationship esteem (i.e., confidence in the partner)
- Good relationship quality
- High responsiveness between the partners

ADJUSTING TO INTIMATE RELATIONSHIP

Adjusting to intimate relationship is not an easy task. It requires considerable degree of skill and efforts. Adjusting to intimate relationships require "couple adjustment", which refers to changes and adjustments in a couple's relationship during the course of their relationship or married life. Couple adjustments require dealing with following issues.

1. Sharing Responsibilities
2. Communication and Conflict
3. Making the Relationship Better
4. Sexuality
5. Changes Over Time

We would discuss each of these briefly:

1. Sharing Responsibilities: Partners whether married or not are sharing responsibilities to a greater extent than what was the situation in the past. Role expectations between partners, especially married couples, are becoming more flexible and functional. Some important points with respect to sharing responsibilities which are worth noting are as follows:

- Decision making among couples have become more democratic.
- Large part of the household work is still the primary responsibility of women.
- Men often share household responsibilities such as cooking, looking after children, etc.
- Research studies have shown that when husbands increase the share of the housework, marital quality improves for women but not for men.

2. Communication and Conflict: Communication and Conflict are unavoidable aspects of any close relationship. Couples conflict with each other for variety of reasons:

- Conflict over money.
- Sexual incompatibilities.
- Unrealistic expectations.
- Lack of affection.
- Power struggle.
- Problems related to child rearing.
- In laws.
- Extra marital affairs.
- Habits (such as drug, alcohol, lavish spending, etc)
- Jealousy.
- Communication difficulties.

A few couples often experience failure in communication at a deeper level of sharing feelings, expectations, intentions and personal needs.

3.Making the Relationship Better: Many couples make attempts to make their relationship better. There are many marital conflict prevention programs available. Premarital education is important and has following advantages.

- Higher levels of satisfaction.
- Better commitment to marriage.
- Lower levels of conflict and
- Reduced chances of divorce.

Relationships can become better when one attempts to understand the reasons and nature of conflict. Conflict is an inevitable part of close relationship. It helps individuals learn more about themselves and each other and deepens their relationship.

One type of therapy that has been found to be highly effective for relationship problems is called as ***Emotion Focused Therapy (EFT).*** It is a cognitive therapy that provides a technique for changing basic thoughts and emotional patterns.

Goal: The goal of EFT is to help partners feel securely connected by fostering feelings of safety, accessibility and responsiveness.

Couples are taught active listening skills where one partner can paraphrase what the other has said, in order to encourage a better relationship environment between them. It is presumed that once the feelings of security and responsiveness develops the couple can better process and send clear messages to each other, to see each other's perspective and do collaborative problem solving.

Mediation: It is another technique for making a relationship better. It can be defined as intervention in a conflict by a neutral third party who assists the conflicting partners in managing and resolving their disputes. Mediation is a quick and a speedy alternative to legal battles, especially in cases involving marital disputes, child custody, divorce, etc.

4. Sexuality: Couples today are engaging in sexual intercourse more frequently than what they did in the past. Couples in 20s or 30s indulge 2-3 times a week. They are also open to wider array of sexual practices.

Couples who have been married or have been staying together for a longer period of time have reduced frequency of sex as compared to newly married couples. Some common reasons for this include:

(a) Lack of time or physical energy.
(b) Decline of sexual order because partners have become "accustomed to each other".
(c) Decrease in physical vigor associated with ageing, especially during middle or late adulthood.
(d) Lack of privacy.
(e) Emphasis on quality of sex rather than its frequency.

Extra marital affairs are also growing and are a major problem, among about 50% of the couples. Infidelity is both a cause as well as the consequence of poor marital quality.

5. Changes Over Time: Marital relationship over a period of time may make a couple either "happy" or lead to "lack of happiness". Why are some couples happier as compared to others? It has been observed that couples who are described happier make relationship enhancing attributions for partner's behavior. Couples who are unhappy tend to make distress enhancing attributions.

Attributions can be defined as a search for the causes of our own or another person's behavior. There are two types of attributions:

(a) Blaming individuals traits or predispositions (Internal attributions)

(b) External factor such as luck or situational forces (External attributions)

It has been observed that happy and unhappy couples differ with respect to different attributions that they make. For e.g., In happy couples wife may attribute her husbands forgetting her birthday due to his busy schedule and over work (external attributions) whereas in unhappy couples wife may attribute the said forgetting to his uncaring and unrealistic behavior (internal attributions).

Attributions play a huge role in causing and maintaining relationship distress. They also play a role in relationship happiness. Couples need to monitor the attributions they make towards each other early in their relationships. If they feel that they have "distress-maintaining attributions mode", they should talk to each other, decide what they can do to reverse the types of attributions they are making and other appropriate measures.

DIVORCE AND ITS CONSEQUENCES

Divorce can be defined as a legal dissolution of marriage. Divorce rate during last 40 years have more than doubled. Today in Urban India more than 50% of the marriages are ending in divorce. Some of the most common reasons for divorce are as follows:

- Lack of preparation for marriage
- Fading religious values
- Changes in the belief system and changes in the notion that marriage is forever to the idea that the primary goal of marriage is happiness and fulfillment.
- Changes in laws, enactment of new laws that has made divorce easier and has empowered women.

Some important topics related to divorce that we will discuss are as follows:

1. The Divorce Experience
2. Single-Parent Families
3. Remarriage

1. The Divorce Experience: The experience of divorce is unpleasant not only because it is a final cause but also because of the process of obtaining divorce is not easy, as it involves:

- Mutual alienation, i.e., Separation from the partner.
- Visiting the office of the advocate, courts.
- Financial strain, stoppage of resources from spouse.
- Visiting counselor, dealing with child custody, sexuality, psychological problems, etc.
- The partners tend to withdraw emotionally from each other or co-exists with a great deal of mutual antagonism.
- Issues involving settlement of property, money, etc.
- Disapproval and rejection by friends, family members, co-workers, etc.
- Separating oneself from the influence of a former partner and becoming an autonomous social being can be highly difficult process.

The above process in some cases can be highly draining, create stress and cause personal problem and adjustment difficulties. In other cases it is an opportunity for self discovery, learning and self growth. It takes most people 2-3 years to recover fully from the distress of divorce and many do not recover completely.

2. Single Parent Families: Divorce has detrimental effects on children. Many children, after their parent's divorce, are part of single families generally headed by mother. Unmarried women becoming pregnant and giving birth to the child, unmarried women adopting children, have given rise to single parent families. It has been noted that (Maher, 2003) children living with single mothers are six times more likely to live in poverty than are children with married parents. Single mothers also face problems related to unemployment, poverty, housing, etc.

Many single mothers hold dead-end jobs or require public assistance or do not receive their child support.

Children from single parent families face problems such as:

- Dropping out of schools.
- Alcohol and drug abuse.
- Smoking.
- Premarital sex, unwedded pregnancy.

3. Remarriage: One fourth of divorce couples get remarried. In most instances, a divorced person marries another divorced person, probably because they share similar experiences or are of the same age. Research studies indicate that second marriages are even more likely to end in divorce. About 40 percent second marriages end in divorce. At least 06 out of 10 remarriages last, which is higher than the first marriage. Partners from second marriage often benefit from their mistakes in an earlier marriage.

Increasing number of remarriage now involves step children. Majority of remarried couples, have children only from their previous marriage, with no children from the remarriage. Only very small numbers of remarried couples have children of their own in addition to children from previous marriages of both partners. Such families are called blended families.

New parent has to handle stepchildren, especially adolescents and young adults tactfully and gradually. If the new parent, too quickly assumes parental authority, especially in matters of discipline, the children may be resentful.

Remarriages involving children from previous marriage pose special demands on the adults as well as the children.

Questions

1. Write short notes on any two of the following:
   - Changing views on Sexuality
   - Sexual Communication
   - Initiating and Refusing Sex
2. Discuss the different phases of Sexual Response Cycle as given by Masters and Johnson.
3. Write short notes on the following:
   - Individual Differences in Sexuality
   - Sexual Orientation
4. Discuss the different types of Sexual Dysfunctions.
5. Write short notes on the following:
   - Sexually Transmitted Diseases
   - Sexual Victimisation
6. Write a note on Triangular Theory of Love.
7. Discuss the different types of Adjustments required in close (intimate) relationships.
8. Discuss different Attachment Styles.
9. Write a note on 'Divorce and its Consequences.'
10. Write short notes on "Destructive Patterns of Communication".

****

7 Stress

Stress takes a heavy toll on nation's well-being. Stress causes serious financial loss to an economy and national income as a result of increased absenteeism, decreased productivity and increasing medical expenses. Stress is also a major contributor, either directly or indirectly to

- Coronary heart disease
- Cancer
- Lung ailments
- Accidental injuries
- Cirrhosis of the liver
- Suicide

Many of the deleterious effects of stress are due to its effects on the immune system.

The following different types of individuals are more likely to suffer from stress:

- Those having high income and are successful.
- Educated people are more likely to suffer from extreme stress.
- Executives, managers and professionals suffer more heavily from stress then those in other occupations.

UNDERSTANDING STRESS

Understanding stress involves conceptualizing about stress and knowing its different aspects and dimensions.

Conceptualizing Stress: Stress is not difficult to conceptualize. However, we generally tend to overlook the subtle and unclear aspects of stress. In order to conceptualize stress we look for its causes and its effects. One way of conceptualizing stress is to understand the meaning of the word stressors.

Stressors: The term stressors are used to refer to variety of external or internal stimuli that evoke stress in us. The term stressors are used to refer to any situation, object or event that is likely to produce stress in us. Stressors are of two types: Chronic Stressors and Acute Stressors. This classification was given by Douglas and Baum (2001). The following table summarizes the distinction between these two types of Stressors.

Acute Stressors	Chronic Stressors
Acute Stressors are threatening events that have a relatively short duration and time limit. Examples of Acute Stressors include: • Waiting for the results of a . final exam. • Fight with a colleague on some issue. • Water flooding in your area due to heavy rains.	Chronic Stressors are threatening events of long duration and no readily apparent clear endpoint. Examples of Chronic Stressors include: • Repeated and irritiating behavior of your boss. • Having a child who is mentally retarded and bed-ridden. • An alcoholic spouse who is financially dependent upon you, etc.

Definition of Stress: There are many definitions of stress. One of the most common definitions is as follows: "Stress can be defined as the pattern of responses individuals make to events that disturb their equilibrium or exceed coping abilities." We experience stress when there is an increasing demand placed on us. The demand can be by a close family member, a boss, situation in which we find ourselves, increased responsibility imposed on us or by the goals that we set. The demand requires effort and resources (time, energy, etc.) from us, which we may lack. Hence, the stress. When events around us disrupt our usual level of functioning and require us to make an extra effort to re-establish our equilibrium we experience stress.

Stress can be defined as a demand placed on our psychological and physical functioning that threatens an individual's adaptation to a given situation. The term stress is generally used in two senses.

- It is used to refer to the negative feeling and emotions that are generated in us.
- The term is also used to refer to the presence of various stressors, that is, various situations that give rise to stress.

Stress involves 3 things –

- Behavioural reactions
- Physiological responses
- Psychological responses

Role of Perception in Causation of Stress: Stress is a matter of perception. One individual may find a given event to be highly stressful, whereas another individual may perceive it as challenging and motivating but not stressful.

Stress is a multifaceted phenomenon that may have beneficial effects in some cases. According to Hans Selye there are four variations of stress.

- **Distress:** When events have harmful effects.
- **Eustress:** Stress that has stimulating effects and it results in personal growth. E.g. – Certain types of sports. It is a good stress.
- **Hyper stress:** It is an excessive stress, usually occurs when events, including positive ones, pile up and stretch the limits of our adaptability. For Example – Individuals who are already under stress at work and home may experience hyper stress when a terrorist attack occurs.
- **Hypo stress:** It is called as insufficient stress. It is apt to occur when we lack stimulation. Monotonous jobs typically give rise to hypo stress.

Chronic Stress v/s Acute Stress: Chronic Stress is also called as globalized or generalized or pervasive stress. It refers to a long lasting and relatively permanent type of stress. Most medical professionals consider this type of stress to be very harmful. Acute stress is one that is a momentary response to imminent danger and is relieved when the danger is over.

Life Changes and Stress: Many life changes result in stress. Long ago Holmes and Rahe (1967) pointed out that negative life events, such as the loss of a job or the death of a loved one is highly stressful. They also observed that even positive events are highly stressful such as joining a professional course or getting married.

The effects of stress largely depend upon the total impact of various life changes - both positive and negative. The amount of readjustment required to deal with a given situation also greatly determines how we respond to stress.

Holmes and Rahe (1967) developed the ***Social Readjustment Rating Scale (SRRS)*** to measure life changes. In this scale there are 43 life events, which reflect the different degrees of readjustments required by each change.

Holmes and Rahe also found that changes in life intensity, i.e., how intensely life events impact us, influence the onset of various illnesses. Stress of Life Events lead to following illness:

- Sudden cardiac death
- Stroke
- Diabetes
- Depression
- Everyday cold
- Flare up of multiple sclerosis

Limitations:

- There are Individual Differences as to how we react to Stress.
- Some events on different occasion may differ with regard to intensity of stress. A given event on one occasion may be perceived to be highly stressful but the same event on another occasion is perceived to be less stressful.

Hassles: It is stress that arises as a result of everyday difficulties, such as:

- Spending money.
- Seriously stuck in a traffic jam.
- Arguments with a bus driver or a rickshaw driver.
- Confrontation with the boss.
- Breakdown of an old car.
- Nagging wife, etc.

One study showed that the most frequent daily Hassles of college students include wasting time, being lonely, and worrying about meeting high achievement standards (Kanner *et. al.*, 1981). Some other hassles of daily life include

- Waiting for bus/train.
- Shopping for Diwali or other such festivals.

- Misplacing an important book, which you had borrowed from your college professor.

Hassles are the minor irritations and constant naggings of everyday life. Daily hassles are the little annoyances that occur practically everyday, such as having to make decisions, arguing with friends and family, trying to meet deadlines at school or work, and stepping on a piece of bubble gum that someone carelessly spat.

Lazarus found that daily hassles have a greater effect on our moods and health than do the major misfortunes of our life.

- People vary considerably in terms of what bothers them.
- The most commonly reported hassle by the college students are anxiety over tests and grades.
- Middle aged people are concerned with their health and money.
- Professional people feel that they have too much to do and not enough time to do it and have difficulty in relaxing.

Lazarus, found that people who experience frequent intense hassles have the poorest health.

Stress and You: Many factors related to oneself is closely associated with stress.

(i) Perception of Stress: One's perception of stress considerably influences the experience of stress. For e.g., some people take criticism of their work as a personal attack and become highly distressed. They also waste a lot of time and energy defending themselves. Others view criticism as a challenge to improve their work. These individuals experience less stress.

(ii) Personal Temperament: One's personal makeup (i.e., temperament) also considerably influences the experience of stress. Those individuals who have inner doubts, low self-esteem and suspiciousness find the demands of everyday life to be more stressful as compared to others.

(iii) Age and Gender: Experience of stress is also considerably influenced by one's age and gender. In general, women and young individuals; especially those appearing for Board exams are more likely to report higher levels of stress as compared to others.

(iv) Personality Traits: Experience of stress is also considerably influenced by one's personality traits, especially,

Neuroticism and Type A personality. Considerable research has been done with respect to relationship between Type A personality and stress.

Type A individuals are more likely to experience stress-related illnesses. Type A individuals are more likely to experience increased levels of stress because of their characteristics such as:

- Competitive
- Argumentative
- Time urgency
- Ambitious
- Hostile
- They judge themselves and others by rigorous standards.

Due to above characteristics, Type A individuals keep themselves under constant stress. They are also more likely to develop heart diseases.

(v) How people react to us?The ways in which others react to us also create stress in us.If you are a victim of prejudice, you are more likely to experience stress.

(vi) Situational Factors: Many situational factors contribute to experiences of stress, some of which are as follows:

- Physical stressors such as too much to do or too many demands on our time and attention.
- Lack of control over decision and demands, both in our personal life and work life.
- Unpredictability of events, especially for which we are not prepared.
- Lack of social support from family and friends.
- Poor interpersonal relations with family members, friends, co-workers, etc.
- Role conflict in which one role (promotion on a job) conflicts with another role (becoming a parent).
- Career concerns including finding a job, receiving a promotion, etc.
- Unpleasant or dangerous conditions such as noisy work environment.

REACTIONS TO STRESS

We react to stress in wide variety of ways. Some of the most common reactions to stress are briefly outlined in the following table:

- Nervousness, anxiety and tension are most common reactions to stress.
- Tension headaches.
- Display of anger and irritability towards others, especially when a demand is made.
- Fatigue and depression are other common reactions to stress.
- Muscle aches, stomach-aches, overall feeling of being upset, etc.
- Loss of sleep, insomnia, loss of appetite.
- Feeling of frustration, crying, yelling and screaming.
- Our body responds to stress in wide variety of ways. Three important physiological reactions to stress are as follows:

(a) People under stress have more heart attacks and strokes,
(b) They catch more colds, and
(c) Respond less to the vaccines.

Physiological Stress Reactions: Hans Selye was a pioneer of stress who found that our body responds to stress in various ways. He found that in addition to body's specific responses to particular stressors (i.e., sweating in response to heat) there also is a characteristic pattern of non-specific physiological mechanisms that are activated in response to every stressor. Selye called this pattern the General Adaptation Syndrome.

General Adaptation Syndrome. It consists of three progressive stages:

1. Alarm Reaction
2. Stage of Resistance
3. Stage of Exhaustion

We would discuss each of these briefly.

1. Alarm Reaction: It is the body's reaction to any threat in the environment. During alarm reaction the body gets alarmed for flight or fight reaction. During the alarm reaction there are number of autonomic nervous system changes as follows:

(a) Increased heartbeat.
(b) Respiration rate.
(c) Blood pressure.
(d) Diversion of blood away from digestion and into the skeletal muscles.

(e) Increased perspiration.

(f) Endocrine glands release epinephrine and other hormones into the blood stream.

(g) Level of blood sugar increases and

(h) Many hormonal changes also take place.

Besides these physical changes, a number of psychological changes also accompany these physical changes. Some of these psychological changes are muscle tension, stomach-aches, headaches, and other feelings of "sickness".

These changes help the organism to either face the stressful situation or to run away from it. Alarm reaction consists of two phases:

(a) Shock phase in which autonomic nervous system changes take place suddenly.

(b) Counter shock phase where body temporarily recovers from the shock phase.

2. Stage of Resistance: During this stage human organism develop an increased resistance to stressors.

3. Stage of Exhaustion: This stage is reached if exposure to stress continues for too long. Hans Selye originally held that the stress response occurs in reaction to various stressors, including illness. However, his theory also relates how a chronic stress reaction can itself lead to illness and accentuate ageing. Continued stress responses use up the body's store of adaptive energy.

Fight or Flight Response: This reaction was first described by Walter Cannon (1932) and it occurs in the body's Autonomic Nervous System (ANS). The flight-or-fight response is a physiological reaction to threat that mobilizes an organism for attacking (fight) or fleeing (flight) an enemy. Flight means fleeing from the stressor. We indulge in flight response when stressor is insurmountable. When it is capable of being overcome we fight it. Stress response begins in the brain. The important areas of the brain involved in fight or flight response are as follows:

(a) Amygdala (which directs signal traffic in the brain and triggers an all-system alarm).

(b) Pituitary gland (the master gland of the endocrine or hormonal system).

Individual's body responds by increasing the flow of various hormones such as adrenaline and cortisol. Similarly, nerve cells release and respond to various neurotransmitters. These changes bring wide range of physiological and biochemical changes in the body.

Prolonged exposure to stress can turn against our body because of elevated levels of physiological functioning. One of the reasons that protracted stress is harmful to our body is because of its prolonged functioning at optimal levels. Chronic elevation can reduce the effectiveness of immune system making it susceptible to many illnesses including cancer.

Allostasis and Allostatic Load: These two concepts were introduced by McEven (2005). Allostosis means achieving stability through changes via a process that maintains balance among the physiological factors essential for life, such as body temperature, blood pressure, heart rate and oxygen level.

Allostatic load refers to cumulative changes that reflect the cost to the body of adapting repeatedly to demands (i.e., stress) placed upon it. According to experts (McEven, Almeida 2005) over the short run, bodily functions associated with allostasis provides protective effects against stress, but over the long run stressors can have damaging effects and adversely affect our life by resulting in poorer health. In other words allostasis helps us physiologically to manage stress but chronic allostatic overload is damaging to our health.

Psychological Stress Reactions: Our psychological reactions to stress are results of our learning. One important psychological reaction to stress is defense mechanisms.

Defense Mechanism: It is also called as "ego defense" mechanisms because the defense mechanisms are used to protect oneself from the perceived threat. According to many Psychologists, including Freud, Defense mechanisms are automatic unconsciousness mechanisms that protect us from the awareness of anxiety, thereby helping us to maintain a sense of self-worth in the face of threat. Some important defense mechanisms are briefly outlined in the following table:

Defense Mechanism	Explanation of Defense Mechanisms
Repression	Excluding unacceptable ideas or feelings from consciousness.
Denial	Misperceiving threatening objects or events as harmless.
Fixation	Fixation means an arrest in development.
Regression	Return to an earlier and more comfortable developmental level.Returning to forms of behavior that are indicative of an earlier level of development such as childhood (usually in response to an overwhelming stressor). For e.g. Raju began sucking his thumb after the birth of his baby sister.
Rationalization	Justifying our unacceptable behavior with "good" reasons.
Intellectualization	Reducing anxiety by analyzing threatening issues in an emotionally detached way.
Projection	Attributing our unacceptable ideas or feelings to others.
Displacement	Redirecting threatening ideas or impulses into less threatening objects.
Sublimation	Sublimation is a process by which socially unacceptable and undesirable sexual and aggressive instincts are expressed in socially acceptable ways.
Acting out	Relieving anxiety or unpleasant tensions by expressing them in overt behavior.
Reaction formation	Defending against unacceptable feelings and behavior by exhibiting the opposite of one's true wishes or impulses.

Since defense mechanisms involve self-deception and a distortion of social reality, habitual reliance on them can prove maladaptive and can stifle personal growth.

Stress can be motivating in few cases. Stress also makes us emotional and thereby our reactions are considerably influenced as to what type of emotions we experience and with what level of sensitivity. Some important points worth noting are as follows:

- Mild stress can energize us to become more alert, active and resourceful.
- Medium stress tends to have disruptive effect on our lives, especially on complex behaviors such as writing the term paper.
- Very high levels of stress can be extremely troublesome. Under such stress, people become less sensitive to their surroundings, easily irritated and more apt to resort to unhealthy coping devices such as consuming too much alcohol or not getting enough sleep.

- Stress also involves a wide range of emotions ranging from a sense of exhilaration in the face of minor challenging stressors to the more familiar negative emotions of anxiety, anger, fear, jealousy, etc.
- Severe stress tends to inhibit behavior and may lead to apathy and immobility.
- One type of reaction to stress is called as Posttraumatic Stress Disorder (PTSD) such type of reactions is generally displayed by survivors of traumatic events such as rape victims, terrorist's hostages, etc.

Posttraumatic Stress Disorder (PTSD): It is a severe anxiety disorder characterized by symptoms of anxiety and avoidance behavior resulting from an unusually distressing event such as being assaulted. PTSD is a severe anxiety disorder that can develop after exposure to a terrifying event. Some events that trigger PTSD are as follows

- Plane crash
- Earthquake
- Floods, hurricanes, tsunami
- Assaults
- Rape
- Hostage taking by terrorists
- Police tortures

How do you react to stress? There are individual differences in how we react to stress. For example:

(a) Some anxious people react with bodily symptoms such as feeling dizzy, having acidity in stomach, splitting headache or having diarrhea.

(b) Some people react to stress physically or psychologically. They become pre-occupied with worries, they are unable to concentrate, have unnecessary fears and thinking too much, few individuals become numb, "stony" or insensitive to their surroundings.

(c) There are gender differences in how we react to stress. Gender differences are seen not only with respect to how we appraise stress but also how individuals cope with it. Women are also known to generate more emotional and social support as compared to men. Women use more emotion focused coping strategy.

The two most important types of coping with stress are as follows:

(a) Emotion Focused Coping: In this form of coping individual tries to alter the emotional reaction to stress by expressing rather than suppressing feelings.

(b) Problem Focused Coping: In this form of coping individual tries to change the environment or find a solution.

Once upon a time emotional focused coping was considered to be less adaptive as compared to problem focused coping. One can deal with stress in a much better manner when one has developed personal grip on stress. Some coping techniques are listed in the table below.

Physical Coping Techniques	Mental (Psychological Coping Techniques)
• Aerobics • Cycling • Walking/jogging • Progressive relaxation • Soaking in hot bath or sauna	• Meditation • Reading • Crossword puzzles • Television • Chess or Card games

Psychological Hardiness: It refers to the attitude that allows them to make the most of the situation. A considerable degree of research in this area has been done by Suzanne Kobasa. She found that those who were "Hardier" were found to be: -

- More committed.
- Felt more in control of the situation.
- Were more oriented to face various types of challenges.

It has been observed that top executives of future 500 companies often show traits of hardiness that help them to cope better with stress.

Resilience: It can be defined as positive growth or positive adaptation following brief periods of stress after some stressful disruption or extreme adversity. Resilient individuals bounce back from stressful experiences quickly and effectively. Such people use:

(i) Humor

(ii) Positive emotions

(iii) Cognitive flexibility

(iv) Cognitive appraisal

(v) Social support

(vi) Optimism to cope with adversity

MANAGING STRESS

Managing stress means taking charge directly and controlling our responses to stressors thereby modifying the overall stress. Managing stress falls under two broad categories.

(A) Modifying Your Environment

(B) Altering Yourself/or Your Response

We would discuss each of them briefly.

(A) Modifying Your Environment: There are many different ways of modifying one's environment. Three most common techniques of modifying one's environment includes:-

- Assertiveness
- Withdrawal and
- Compromise

These three techniques are considered environmental rather than personal responses to stress because they either change your environment or change the responses of others who are creating stress for you.

Assertiveness: Assertiveness is the preferred way to manage stress whenever there is a reasonable possibility of success. It is the expression of one's rights and feelings in a direct way without violating the rights of others. Such an approach consists of direct attempts at modifying the stressful situation itself. For example:

(a) Returning a defective product to a store.

(b) Speaking up in response to an unreasonable request.

Assertiveness is a rational and constructive way of handling stress, which in turn tends to alleviate the stress involved.

Withdrawal: It means removing oneself physically and emotionally from an activity, organization or person. Withdrawal may be appropriate response to stress, especially when a stressful situation cannot be successfully modified through assertiveness or compromise. Withdrawal is neither good nor bad in itself; much depends on how it is used. If someone habitually withdraws from stressful situation, then that person may drift into constructed lifestyle that prevents adequate adjustments or personal growth.

Compromise: It is another adaptive response to stress and occurs when an adjustment is made by modifying opposing ideas or behaviors. The three most important types of compromise are:

(a) Conformity
(b) Negotiation
(c) Substitution

Conformity as response to stressful situations involves a change in our behavior due to other's direct influence. It occurs in situations where individuals change their behaviour in order to adhere to widely accepted standards or beliefs (often termed social norms). It is also defined as behaving in ways that are viewed as acceptable or appropriate in our group or society. Pressure to conform is very hard to resist and often we conform even when we are not willing to conform.

Negotiation is a more active and promising way to achieve compromise in many stressful situations. Negotiations mean that we make mutual concessions with another person.

Substitution: It means that we seek alternative goals with another person. For example: if you do not get admission to a course of your choice you can decide to do an alternative course.

Compromise itself is neither good nor bad. More depends on the relation between the satisfaction achieved and the price paid for the reduction of stress. Habitual compromise may bring more frustration and conflict.

(B) Altering Yourself/or Your Response, i.e., Altering Your Lifestyle: Individuals can learn to manage stress by altering their lifestyles. Some common techniques of altering one's lifestyle are as follows:

(a) Developing greater stress tolerance.
(b) Altering our everyday habits.
(c) Learning to control distressing thoughts.
(d) Acquiring problem solving skills.
(e) Seeking social support.

We would discuss each of these briefly

(a) Developing greater stress tolerance: Stress tolerance can be defined as the amount of stress you can handle or how long you can put up with a demanding task without acting in an irrational or disorganized way. Many successful people who experience stress have learned to tolerate greater amounts of stress. Greater tolerance comes with greater experience and skill. We can increase our tolerance by:

- Selecting reasonable goals and adjusting our expectations to match the realities of the immediate situation.
- Increasing our ability to function well despite anxiety.

(b) Altering our everyday habits: In order to reduce stress we need to alter our everyday habits including changing our pace of life. You might be bringing a lot of stress on yourself by rushing around and trying to accomplish too much in too little time. A fast pace of life makes one walk, talk, conduct your business and do almost everything faster. This causes considerable physical and mental stress. It has been observed that individuals who feel time pressure, experience blood pressure that is much higher than individuals who do not put themselves under pressure. Some important steps that can help us to change our habits and slowdown the paces of life are as follows:

(i) Get up early to avoid rushing.

(ii) Listen to music.

(iii) Take time for breakfast.

(iv) Make a list of things to do, put the most important things first.

(v) Allow enough time to drive to school or work without rushing.

(vi) Walk at an unhurried pace.

(vii) Share meal each day with another people.

(viii) Avoid excessive use of alcohol, drugs, caffeine, etc.

(ix) Take time to walk, relax, ride bicycles, etc.

(x) Unplug phone.

(xi) Have a contingency plan if things go wrong.

(xii) Set regular time for study or certain essential work.

(xiii) Jot down things you have not done today but would like to do it tomorrow.

(c) Learning to control distressing thoughts: We often experience and bring distressing thoughts to our minds. Imagine writing an exam paper. The first two questions, from the question paper which you have just glanced, are found to be difficult, now you may mutter to yourself: "If the rest of the paper is this hard, I am going to flunk". We often indulge in such negative self-talk which often generates stress in us. You can overcome your negative thoughts in following ways:

- Become aware of your negative thoughts, you will realize that negative thoughts are unrealistic and make you draw wrong inferences.
  - (a) "I will never make it"
  - (b) "How did I get into this mess?"
  - (c) Why should I only have trouble? Etc.
  - (i) Formulate thoughts that are incompatible with your distressful thoughts for e.g.,
  - (ii) "I can do it, just take one step at a time"
  - (iii) " I will keep doing my best to see how things turn out"
- Replace your distressing thoughts with humorous thoughts.
- Learn to joke, laugh, recall funny events, etc.

(d) Acquiring problem solving skills: Many individuals experience stress because they lack problem solving skills. These skills come through guidance, experience and learning.

(e) Seeking social support: Having access to friends and support groups may help to alleviate stress in many ways:

- Close relationship provide the opportunity to share painful feelings which if kept to ourselves become more burdensome.
- Friends provide emotional support through their expressions of concern and affection.
- Assurance of our friends may boost up our self-esteem throughout the low periods of our lives.
- Friends and support groups may provide information and advice that may help us to reach more effective solutions to our problems.
- Friends can enhance positive experiences in our lives.

It should be remembered that some people who are close to us can give us more stress, such people are called as "toxic people". These may include:

- judgmental spouse
- A friend who constantly ask for favors
- Difficult boss

People who have access to close and supportive relationships enjoy greater emotional and physical health than those without close social ties.

Using Stress for Personal Growth: Stress can enhance personal growth and can be valuable means of self-understanding. Some important points with respect to using stress for personal growth are as follows:

- We don't fully know that what we can do until we have to do it.
- Each time we successfully get through a stressful situation, like a difficult course at a school or having problem in personal life, we gain in self-control.
- Each experience of disappointment and failure are sometimes blessings in disguise. Sometimes a minor failure today can save us from a bigger let down in future life.
- We can make stress work for us. Remember that stress is not synonymous with "distress" or 'stressed out". Too little stress can make us feel bored and lazy. Increased levels of stress can make us tense, make us commit more mistakes and get sick easily.
- To get most out of life, each of us needs to determine, our optimal level of handling stress. If properly managed, stress can give zest to life. A stressful situation can challenge us to try harder, evoking our best response and bring personal growth.

Questions

1. Write notes on the following:
   (a) Role of Perception in causation of Stress
   (b) Life Changes and Stress
   (c) Chronic v/s Acute Stressors
   (d) Hassles
2. Discuss the various Physiological and Psychological reactions to Stress.
3. Write notes on the following:
   (a) General Adaptation Syndrome
   (b) Allostasis and Allostatic Load
   (c) Defense Mechanisms
   (d) Psychological Hardiness and Resilience
4. Discuss the different techniques of Managing Stress.
5. Write notes on the following:
   (i) Using Stress for Personal Growth.

****

8 Understanding Mental Disorders

Mental disorders are also called as psychological disorders. They also include anxiety disorders, mood disorders, cognitive disorders and other common disorders, such as eating disorders, personality disorders, schizophrenia, etc.

PSYCHOLOGICAL DISORDERS

Psychological disorders refers to a group of disorders which have been labeled in different ways from time to time. Some individuals, especially layman may use the terms "nervous breakdown" or "abnormal behavior", "psychological problem", "mental disorder", etc., to refer to Psychological Disorders.

Study of psychological disorder is closely associated with the study of abnormal behavior. It should be remembered that all psychological disorders are not abnormal behaviors.

The term psychological disorder has been defined as a clinically significant behavioral or psychological pattern that is associated with

(a) Present personal distress.

(b) Disability or impairment in one or more important areas of functioning, e.g., maladaptive behavior.

(c) Significantly increased risk of suffering disability, pain or death and

(d) An important loss of freedom or personal control.

Characteristic of Psychological Disorders: Some of the most important characteristics of a given psychological disorder are as follows:

(i) **Personal Distress:** An individual is said to experience psychological disorder when he/she experiences personal distress. We can define personal distress as intense or chronic negative self-awareness that interferes with one's sense of well being or functioning. An individual with a chronic fear of heights or a marked change in mood, such as severe depression, might be diagnosed as having a psychological disorder. If an individual behaves in an unusual or eccentric way, but he/she is otherwise happy, then he/she would not be diagnosed as having a psychological disorder.

(ii) **Maladaptive Behavior:** It refers to disability or impairment in one or more important areas of psychological functioning, especially the ability to work and get along with others. People with psychological disorders usually suffer from a significant impairment in their:

(i) Ability to work.

(ii) To care for themselves

(iii) And to get along with friends and family

(iii) **Increased Risk of Suffering Disability Pain or Death:** Individuals suffering from psychological disorder are at increased risk of suffering from disability pain or death. They may not maintain a healthy diet; take care of physical health which may make them prone to many problems making their adjustment difficult.

(iv) **Loss of Freedom or Personal Control:** Individuals suffering from psychological disorders often experience loss of freedom or personal control. They feel that they are not free to decide what to do and have no control either on their own lives or over behaviour of others. It should be remembered that social norms play an important role in causation of psychological disorders.

How common are Psychological Disorders? Psychological disorders are very common form of disorder throughout the world. Mental disorders rank second after cardiovascular diseases. According to the recent study, mental health professionals have estimated that one in four adults suffer from some type of psychological disorder. Symptoms of certain disorders such as alcohol abuse, obsessive-compulsive behavior, bipolar disorders and schizophrenia appear somewhat earlier at a median age of 20 years. Some important points with respect to psychological disorders worth noting are as follows:-

(a) Men and women are equally likely to suffer from psychological disorders.

(b) Patterns of disorders differ somewhat between the sexes.

(c) Frequencies of mental disorder varies from culture to culture.

(d) Women suffer from phobias (intense and irrational fear) and men are likely to suffer from alcohol, drug abuse, antisocial bchavior, etc.

(e) Women are twice more likely to seek help as compared to men.

How are Disorders Classified? Psychological disorders are classified in many different ways. One system of classification is the Diagnostic and Statistical Manual of Mental Disorders (DSM) which is currently available in 4th edition (text revision) also called as DSM - IV - TR.

DSM classifies, defines and describes over 200 psychological disorders. While classifying psychological disorder, emphasis is on behavior patterns, not people. DSM gives clinician a practical behavioral approach to dealing with people exhibiting symptoms of psychological disorders.

ANXIETY DISORDERS

Anxiety is a vague, subjective awareness of threat or danger. Anxiety is a mood state consisting of negative effect, apprehension about future, bodily symptoms of tension, etc. It is manifested in human being as a subjective sense of unease, a set of behaviour (such as looking worried and anxious, fidgeting) and a physiological response consisting of changes in heart rate. Anxiety is an unpleasant emotional state. It is a foreboding, a feeling that something bad is about to happen.

One form of anxiety is worry. Anxiety in its many forms tends to function as an emotional alarm signal, warning the individual of threat or imminent danger.

Anxiety arising out of real threat such as loss of job can motivate us to make adaptive adjustments. It motivates us to take the necessary steps to avoid such a misfortune.

Anxiety is a natural emotional response to stress and it is considered as a normal part of life. Anxiety at times can be energizing and motivating, though high levels of anxiety can immobilize us. Individuals with high levels of anxiety may find it hard to concentrate and make decisions.

Types of Anxiety Disorders: Three most important types of anxiety disorders are as follows:

(a) **Generalized Anxiety Disorder:** It is a chronic state of diffuse or free floating anxiety.

(b) **Phobic Disorder:** Intense anxiety generated by some specific and irrational object or activity.

(c) **Obsessive-Compulsive Disorder:** Involuntary dwelling on an unwelcome thought or the involuntary repetition of unnecessary actions.

(a) Generalized Anxiety Disorder: The main characteristic of generalized anxiety disorder is a persistent sense of "free floating" anxiety. People who are chronically anxious can't say what they are afraid of. All they know is that they feel on the edge all the time. They generally worry a lot and anticipate the occurrence of something bad. In this disorder people also experience panic attacks which is characterized by the occurrence of severe panic. The intense attacks occur in the absence of a feared situation and usually last 15-20 minutes. In some case the attack occur in response to a specific situation, such as driving in city traffic or speaking publicly. In a panic attack, anxiety increases to almost intolerable levels. Panic attacks usually last for few seconds, but may continue for hours. Afterwards the victims feel exhausted. Panic attacks are unpredictable and that also creates anxiety in an individual. He/she thinks what will happen if I get panic attack?

(b) Phobic Disorders: Phobia is an irrational fear in which an individual avoids an object or a situation. It is a persistent and disproportionate fear of some specific object of situation that presents little or no actual danger to a person. Phobic disorders are characterized by a persistent and irrational fear of a specific object or activity accompanied by a compelling desire to avoid it. Most of us experience an irrational avoidance of selected objects like spiders, snakes, rats, etc. We make diagnosis of phobic disorder when our avoidance of objects and events become a source of distress and interfere with our everyday functioning. There are many different types of phobia. The three most common types of Phobia are as follows:

- Simple phobia
- Social phobia

- Agoraphobia

Simple Phobias are the most common types of phobia. It is the fear of common objects such as animals especially dogs, snakes, insects, etc.

Two most common types of simple phobia are as follows.

- **Acrophobia:** Fear of heights.
- **Claustrophobia:** Fear of closed places.

Most simple phobias originate in childhood and disappear without treatment. Most intense fear that originates in childhood generally doesn't disappear without treatment.

Social phobia: It is an extreme form of shyness that can interfere with an individual's daily life and involves a chronic irrational fear of and a compelling desire to avoid situations where others may scrutinize an individual. Some examples of social phobia include the following:

- Intense fear of speaking or performing in public.
- Eating in public.
- Using public lavatories.
- Writing in the presence of others.

Agoraphobia: It is the fear of open space. It is a cluster of different fears, all of which evoke intense anxiety about crowds or open space such as:

- crowded storey.
- elevators or tunnels.
- public transportation.

This type of phobia tends to occur in late teens or early twenties though it can occur later in life.

(c) Obsessive Compulsive Disorder: It involves involuntary dwelling on an unwelcome thought or the involuntary repetition of an unnecessary act. It is sometimes called as "doubting disease". This disorder involves two separate disorders.

(i) Obsession: It is a thought or image that keeps recurring in the mind, despite an individual's attempt to ignore it or resist it.

(ii) Compulsion: It is an act that individual feels compelled to repeat again and again usually in ritualistic fashion and according to certain rules. The act is performed with a sense of compulsion, coupled with a desire to resist such action, at least initially. The individual usually realizes that the behavior is senseless and does not derive pleasure from carrying it out, though doing so provides a release of tension.

OCD: It is thought to be caused by disruption of the basal ganglia of the brain, which is a region in the brain that filters messages. Most of us experience minor obsessions, which are generally temporary and do not interfere with everyday activities. In contrast pathological obsessions reoccur day-after-day. They sometimes involve thoughts of lust and violence. For example:

- Fear of being contaminated by germs.
- Fear that one will kill one's child/spouse.
- The temptation to have sex with forbidden partner.

There are pathological types of compulsion which are as follows:

- **Hoarders:** who collect almost everything and cannot get rid of it.
- **Repeaters:** who believe they must repeat a behavior number of times.
- **Orderers:** who want their possessions in certain places and arranged in certain ways.

Trauma and Disaster: These two forms of disorder have received increased attention in recent years, from psychologists. One type of such behavior is called as **Posttraumatic Stress Disorder (PTSD).** It is a severe anxiety disorder characterized by symptoms of anxiety and avoidance behavior. This disorder results from an unusually stressful event such as being assaulted. PTSD can be caused due to following factors:

- devastation due to war.
- natural disaster.
- sniper attack.
- rapes.
- plane crashes.
- terrorists attacks.
- car accidents.
- murders, etc.

Most cases of PTSD involve life threatening events.

Symptoms of PTSD: Some common symptoms of PTSD are as follows:

(i) Intense fear, flashbacks and thinking about the events again and again.
(ii) Nightmares.
(iii) Mood swings, irritability, depression, sadness, crying, etc.
(iv) Limited attention span, difficulty in concentrating and confusion.
(v) Physical symptoms such as headaches, sleep disturbances, stomach-aches, etc.
(vi) Guilt and self-doubt.
(vii) Fear of crowds, strangers, being alone.
(viii) Difficulty in communicating thoughts.

Certain groups of people are more prone to PTSD, these include:

- Police personnel.
- Victims who narrowly escape deaths.
- Energizing rescue workers.
- Those who have already lost a loved one.
- Women are more likely, as compared to men, to suffer from PTSD.
- Children are more vulnerable than adults, especially, if they have been abused or are suffering from chronic stress.

Overcoming PTSD: PTSD can be overcome in following ways:

(i) Talk to someone about your feelings.
(ii) Spend time with family and friends.
(iii) Do not hold yourself responsible for the event or for not responding sooner or later.
(iv) Staying active in your daily routine, it helps to overcome many symptoms of PTSD.
(v) Seek professional help.
(vi) Visit religious places, attend religious functions, etc.

MOOD DISORDERS

Mood disorders are a group of disorders which involve mood disturbances including extreme elation and depression, seasonal affective disorder, suicide, bipolar disorder, etc. Some of the most common mood disorders which we would discuss in brief are as follows:

1. Depression
2. Seasonal Affective Disorder
3. Suicide
4. Bipolar Disorder

1. Depression: It is an emotional state characterized by intense and unrealistic sadness that may assume a variety of forms, some more severe and chronic than others. Depression is so common in our life that it is often referred to as the "common cold of mental illness". Depression can range from mild crying to suicidal attempts. Some common symptoms of depression include

(i) decreased energy.
(ii) loss of interest in everyday activities.
(iii) pessimistic attitude.
(iv) in extreme forms of depression, hallucinations or delusions may be present.

Depression is a result of multiple causes, some of which are biological and genetic in nature. It can also be triggered by the stress of student life such as:

- academic pressures
- making career decisions
- financial difficulties
- family problems, such as parental divorce.

According to cognitive psychologists, depression is caused by negative thinking and pessimistic cognitive styles.

2. Seasonal Affective Disorder (SAD): The term Seasonal Affective Disorder (SAD) is used to refer to a mood disorder involving a cycling of episodes corresponding to the seasons of the year, typically with depression occurring during winter. People with winter depression tend to sleep excessively and increase weight and appetite. It has also been found that SAD is related to daily and seasonal changes in the production of melatonin, a hormone secreted by the pineal gland. It has been found that melatonin production tends to increase in winter.

Symptoms of SAD: It may consist of difficulty of waking up in the morning, tendency to oversleep as well as to overeat, and especially a craving for carbohydrates, which leads to weight gain. Other symptoms include a lack of energy, difficulty in concentrating on completing tasks, and withdrawal from friends, family, and social activities. All of this leads to the depression, pessimism, and lack of pleasure which characterizes a person suffering from this disorder.

3. Suicide: It involves killing oneself. It is the most common type of behavior that is closely related to depression. Every suicide may not be due to depression. Suicide has been found to be very common among different societies; some have described it as a disease of civilization.

Causes of suicide: Some of the most common reasons for suicide are as follows:

- escaping from pain or stress.
- trying to eliminate unacceptable feelings.
- turning aggression inwards.
- punishing others by making them feel guilty.
- acting impulsively or momentary feelings of desperation.
- suicidal people also experience "tunnel vision"— the mis-perception that suicide is the only alternative to unsolvable problems in life.

Suicide prevention programs have received considerable attention in recent years. Prevention of suicide involves:

- tightening control over prescription medicines.
- controlling gun purchases through legislation.
- protective measures such as, putting fencing on high-rise buildings, etc.
- increasing self awareness, community awareness, etc.
- increasing counseling services.
- educating parents.

4. Bipolar Disorder: It was earlier called as Manic-Depressive Disorder. It involves an alteration of elated and depressive moods. This disorder first appears as mania in which an individual exhibits some of the following symptoms:

- Expansive mood.
- Increased social activity.
- Sleeplessness.
- Reckless behavior.
- Talkativeness.

The initial manic episode may be followed by periods of normal activity, followed by a depressed episode and then another normal period. Or one mood may be followed immediately by its opposite, with intervals of normal functioning. In rare forms, the person's mood may alternate between manic and depressive episodes, with no intervals of normal functioning. In another rare form, the mixed type, the individual may experience symptoms of both moods simultaneously.

In additional to manic episodes there are other characteristics that distinguish bipolar disorder from major depression.

- Bipolar disorder is much less common than major disorder.
- Bipolar disorder is equally prevalent among men and women.
- Unlike major depression which occurs more frequently among the lower socio-economic classes, bipolar disorder is more prevalent among the upper classes.
- Although married people are less susceptible to major depression, they enjoy no such advantages in regard to bipolar disorder.
- Although major depression can occur at any time in life, bipolar disorder usually appears before the age of 30.
- Bipolar episodes tend to be briefer and more frequent than those in major depression.
- Bipolar disorders are more likely to run in families.

OTHER COMMON DISORDERS

There are many other common disorders which are difficult to list.

Three most common disorders are as follows.

1. Eating Disorders
2. Personality Disorders
3. Schizophrenia

We would discuss each of these briefly.

1. Eating Disorder: Eating Disorders are characterized by abnormal eating habits that may involve either insufficient or excessive food intake which can damage an individual's physical and emotional health. Generally, eating disorders involve self-critical, negative thoughts and feelings about body weight and food, and eating habits that disrupt normal body function and daily activities.

Types of Eating Disorders: The three most common types of eating disorders are as follows:

- Anorexia Nervosa
- Bulimia Nervosa
- Binge Eating

Anorexia Nervosa: An eating disorder characterized by a severe loss of appetite and weight. The essential feature of this eating disorder is a fear of becoming fat along with a disturbance of body image and a refusal to maintain normal weight. Those individuals who suffer from this disorder relentlessly pursue thinness.

Bulimia Nervosa: An eating disorder characterized by excessive overeating or uncontrolled binge eating followed by self–induced vomiting. The essential feature of this disorder are episodic eating accompanied by an awareness that this eating pattern is abnormal - a fear of not being able to stop eating voluntarily and depressed mood and self-disparaging thoughts. Individuals, who suffer from bulimia, sometimes diet excessively between binges. Bulimia is more common among girls, especially those in the middle and upper socio-economic groups.

Binge Eating: It is also called as compulsive eating. It is characterized by eating excessive amounts of food within a discrete period of time and by a severe lack of control over eating during episodes. Binge eaters consume large amounts of food in a very short period of time. About one-third or more of all individuals in weight-control programs report frequent episodes of compulsive overeating. Compulsive overeaters exhibit a higher–than-average incidence of psychological problems, especially depression. Compulsive overeaters also tend to experience greater mood fluctuation during the day. Binge eating is commonly triggered by tension, hunger, boredom, craving for specific food, etc.

2. Personality Disorders: Personality disorders occur when we possess inflexible and maladaptive behavior or personality traits that causes marked impairment in individual's social and occupational life.

Personality disorders are generally long-lasting and results in pattern of deviation from accepted social norms. Individuals suffering from this disorder should seek professional help. There are more than 11 different types of personality disorders according to DSM. The three most important common forms of personality disorders are as follows:

- Narcissistic Personality Disorder
- Antisocial Personality Disorder
- Borderline Personality Disorder

We will discuss each of them briefly:

(i) Narcissistic Personality Disorder: It is a disorder characterized by an undue sense of self importance often accompanied by a sense of inferiority. Psychologists differ about the causes of narcissistic personality disorder.

- Psychodynamic (Freudian) theorists believe that narcissistic personalities compensate for the inadequate affection and approval they received in childhood.
- Cognitive and social learning theorists see narcissistic people as products of exaggerated expectations during childhood of what they will achieve in adulthood.

(ii) Anti-social Personality Disorder: This disorder is characterized by longstanding habits of maladaptive thoughts and behavior that violate the rights of others. Individuals with this disorder were earlier called as Psychopathic or Sociopathic Personality. Some important characteristic of this disorder are as follows:

- These people have a family history of chronic antisocial behavior.
- They disregard other's rights.
- They tend to get in trouble with the law.
- They act in impulsive manner.
- They are irresponsible and often walk out of their jobs or spouses.
- Anti-social personalities lack normal conscience, are manipulative towards others, have no guilt, etc.

(iii) Borderline Personality Disorder: Individuals having this disorder show:

(a) Impulsive behavior.

(b) Unstable social relationships and

(c) Unstable self-image.

Their impulsiveness is often self-damaging leading to suicidal behavior, threats, self-mutilation, etc. These individuals often display unstable mood, with intense or inappropriate episodes of irritability, anxiety, euphoria, etc. These individuals are highly demanding, even from psychotherapists and often indulge in assaultive and aggressive behavior with their loved ones.

3. Schizophrenia: It is the most severe form of mental disorder which is also called as "split personality" by the public. It is a label given to a group of related disorders characterized by:

- Severe disorganization of thoughts, perceptions and emotions.
- Bizarre behavior.
- Social withdrawal.

The essential feature of these disorders includes psychotic symptoms that are signs of psychosis and that include hallucinations such as hearing voices, marked impairment in self-care and social relationships and other signs of severe disturbances. Important symptoms of schizophrenia include:

(a) **Disorder of Speech:** There is a loosening of associations of thought and rambling, disjointed speech.

(b) **Distorted Beliefs:** These are also called as delusions which are beliefs that have no basis in reality.

(c) **Distorted Perceptions:** One type of such perception is called as hallucination, which can be defined as sensory perceptions that occur in the absence of any appropriate external stimulus. The most common hallucination is hearing voices that characteristically order these people to commit suicide or other forbidden crime or act.

(d) **Blunted or Inappropriate Emotions:** Schizophrenia is characterized by a blunted affect (emotion) or in more severe cases a lack of emotion. Schizophrenic individuals may stare with a blank expression or speak in a flat, monotonous voice; they also display inappropriate emotions such as giggling when talking about some painful experience.

(e) **Social withdrawal:** People who have schizophrenia tend to be loners; preferring animals, nature or inanimate objects to human company. Individuals having schizophrenia are also emotionally distant, making it difficult to establish satisfying close relationships with them.

Causes of Schizophrenia: The causes of schizophrenia are not fully understood. Once it was believed that it is a result of dysfunctional family environment. Recent research has pointed out towards increasing evidence that genetic, neurological, and bio-chemical factors play a greater role. One view of causation of schizophrenia is **diathesis-stress hypothesis,** which views schizophrenia as the interaction of a genetic vulnerability with environmental stressors. Schizophrenic individuals tend to inherit a lower threshold to certain types of stress, which, if exceeded, may precipitate an acute episode of the disorder. If an individual manages to keep the level of environmental stress well below a particular threshold and despite a genetic predisposition, that person may never experience an acute episode of schizophrenia.

Questions

1. What are Psychological Disorders? Discuss their characteristics and classification.
2. Discuss the different types of Anxiety Disorders.
3. Write short notes on the following:
   (a) Trauma and Disaster
   (b) Schizophrenia
4. Discuss the different types of Mood Disorders.
5. Explain the different types of Eating Disorders.
6. What are Personality Disorders? Explain any three important Personality Disorders.

****

9 Therapy and Treatment

Psychotherapy and treatment through psychological means has received increasing attention in recent areas even from the medical fraternity.

Psychotherapy is the helping process in which a trained, socially sanctioned, therapist performs certain activities that will facilitate a change in the client's (some still prefer to use the term patient) attitude and behavior.

Psychotherapy refers to psychological methods of behavior and attitude change which are more likely to be used by people with the milder disturbances, who seek it as a means of personal growth as well as for the relief of symptoms.

Psychotherapy is the treatment by psychological means of the problem of an emotional nature in which a trained person deliberately establishes a professional relationship with the patient. In doing so, his objectives are usually as follows:

(i) To remove, to modify or to retard (inhibit) the existing disturbing symptoms,

(ii) To modify disturbed patterns of behavior, and

(iii) To promote positive personality development and growth.

"Psychotherapy includes a multitude of psychological methods all of which have one thing in common and that is, the intent to help the mentally suffering individual, though psychological means."

Seeking help of a psychotherapist or even other related non-professionals is not an easy task. It involves:

(a) Increasing one's awareness.
(b) Finding a good therapist.
(c) Spending time and money as well as doing regular follow-up.
(d) Most important is putting into practice what has been advised by the psychologist.
(e) One of the major problems in undergoing psychotherapy is that of choosing a therapist - a person trained to help people with psychological problems. There are total 270 different forms of therapy including various insight therapies and many behavioral and group therapies.
(f) Overcoming one's inhibitions, resistances and prejudices concerning psychology, psychotherapy and mental health.

Goals of Therapy: Most therapies have certain common goals which are as follows:

(i) All of them offer clients relief from their symptoms such as intolerable anxiety or depression.
(ii) Many of them offer clients better understanding of their thoughts, feelings, and relationships.
(iii) They also help clients modify their problem behaviors such as excessive fears, phobias, etc.
(iv) Many therapies also help the clients to improve their interpersonal relationships at home and work.

Different therapies emphasize on different goals. Some put more emphasis on adjustments, whereas others may concentrate on growth or emotional responses.

Types of Therapies: The three most important different types of therapies are as follows:

(i) Insight Therapies
(ii) Cognitive Behavioral Therapies
(iii) Other Approaches to Treatment

We would discuss each of these briefly

Insight Therapies: Some of the most common insight therapies are as follows:

- Psychoanalysis
- The Person-Centered Approach
- Other Approaches

Psychoanalysis: This is the most common insight therapy. This form of therapy is aimed at helping the person gain insight and mastery over unconscious conflicts. Psychoanalysis is Freud's therapeutic technique for analyzing an individual's unconscious thought. Freud believed that client's current problems could be traced to childhood experiences, many of which involved conflicts about sexuality. He also recognized that the early experiences were not readily available to the individual's conscious mind. Only through extensive questioning, probing, and analyzing was Freud able to put the pieces of the individual's personality together and help the individual become aware of how these early experiences were affecting present adult behavior. To reach the shadowy world of the unconscious, psychoanalytic therapists often uses wide variety of therapeutic techniques such as Free association, Catharsis, Dream analysis, Transference, Interpretation and Resistance.

The Person-Centered Approach: It is also called as the Client Centered Therapy or Rogerian therapy. Person Centered Therapy is a form of humanistic therapy developed By Carl Rogers in which the therapist provides a warm, supportive atmosphere to improve the client's self-concept and encourage the client to gain insight about problems.

Carl Rogers emphasized on therapeutic relationship between the client and the therapists. According to him improvement in therapy occurs because the therapists.

- Follow the lead provided by clients.
- Listen and understand their problems.
- Do not impose their diagnostic understanding on clients.
- Responding and respecting the client's own frame of reference.
- Demonstrating to their clients that there exists inherent potential for growth in them.

Conditions for Therapeutic Change: According to Rogers, three essential conditions for bringing change in the clients are as follows:

(i) Genuineness or Congruence.

(ii) Attitude of Acceptance and Caring also called as Unconditional Positive Regard.

(iii) Empathic Understanding.

Other Approaches: There are many different varieties of insight therapies, some of which are listed below:-

(a) Existential Therapy: An approach that emphasizes the client's capacity for growth through affirmation of their free choice and personal values.

(b) Logo Therapy: This approach was developed by Victor Frankl. It stresses on the importance of clarifying those values that give personal meaning and purpose to one's life. Individuals must have:

- The courage to make choice.
- Breakaway from restrictive lifestyles.
- Take responsibility for their lives.

(c) Gestalt Therapy: It was developed by Fritz Perls. This form of therapy emphasises on individual's responsibility in therapy. It makes use of here and now, non verbal behaviour in therapy session as a way of helping clients unify their feelings and actions.

(d) Actualization Therapy: It was developed by Everett Shastrom. This therapy combines elements of the Person Centered Approach, Gestalt Therapy and Rational Emotive Therapy as a way of maximizing the individual's growth or self-actualization.

COGNITIVE-BEHAVIORAL THERAPIES

Cognitive-behavioural Therapies refer to group of therapies whose aim is to bring about changes in behaviour by modifying faulty thinking.

Behavioural Therapies: Behavioural therapies have a long history having originated in the works of B.F.Skinner, Joseph Wolfe and others. Behavioral therapy involves:

- Discovering the factors that trigger and reinforce the problem behaviour.
- Specifying target behaviour to replace it and then manipulating these factors to bring about the desired behavoiur.

Behavioural therapies help the clients to develop the necessary skills or behaviours to cope more effectively with their life situations.

Techniques used by Behaviour Therapies: There are many different techniques used by behavioral therapist, these include:

- Desenstization
- Aversive Counter Conditioning
- Token Economies
- Modeling
- Social Skills Training such as Assertiveness Training.

We would discuss only the desensitization techniques in brief.

Desensitization: This technique was developed by Joseph Wolpe. It is a method of controlling anxiety by learning to associate an incompatible response, like relaxation with the fear provoking stimulus. By linking the feared object or situation to something pleasant, like relaxation, the clients become desensitized to the fearful situation. Desensitization is especially effective with fears and phobias.

Behavioral Rehearsal and *in Vivo* Desensitization: In behavioral rehearsal the client role-plays the feared situation. *In vivo* desentization is also called as real life situation. In this the individual approaches the feared situation directly. It is a method of controlling anxiety by learning to associate an incompatible response, like relaxation, with the fear provoking stimulus.It is often used in the treatment of agrophobia i.e., fear of open spaces.

Cognitive Therapies: Cognitive Therapies are based on the premise that faulty cognitive processes are the cause of problems that individual experiences. These faulty cognitive processes include:

(1) Attention
(2) Perception
(3) Thought
(4) Beliefs

Cognitive Therapies claim people's actions are often shaped more by their own interpretation and reactions to external events than to the events themselves. Two most well known cognitive therapies are as follows:

(i) Rational Emotive Therapy given by Albert Ellis
(ii) Cognitive Therapy developed by Aaron Beck

The central assumption of both these therapies is that the emotional and behavioural problems result from an individual's distorted thoughts and reactions to external events rather than from the events themselves. These approaches encourage people to think more rationally about themselves and their problems. These therapies hold the view that individual's beliefs affect their interpretation and response to various life circumstances, thereby contributing to emotional adjustment/maladjustment.

Cognitive therapist differs from insight therapist in that they do not probe for deep seated causes of the client's problems. Their goal is to identify faulty assumptions and thought patterns and then rely on established behavioural procedures such as behaviour rehearsals or desensitization to alter the behaviour.

OTHER APRROACHES TO TREATMENT

There are many different types of treatment approaches. Some of the treatment approaches that we will discuss in this section are as follows:

(1) Group Therapies
(2) Relationship Therapy
(3) Family Therapy
(4) Biomedical Therapies
(5) Community-based Services

We would discuss this each of these briefly.

1. Group Therapies: Many group therapies have mushroomed in number and type in the past several decades. Groups not only offer opportunities for people to interact with others with similar problems but also are more cost-efficient, saving time and money. One type of group therapy is called as self-help or mutual help groups.

Mutual Help Groups: There are more then 5,00,000 self-help groups in which an estimated 12 million people participate. These are those groups whose member's shares common problems and meet regularly to discuss their concerns without the guidance of professionals. These groups have multiple agenda/ programme:

- Fostering self-help.
- Lobbying for reform.
- To provide social support.

To provide practical help in dealing with problems common to all members.

Mutual-help groups provide an atmosphere of acceptance and support that encourages their members to communicate more openly, view their problems objectively and find more effective coping strategies.

2. Relationship Therapy: Relationship therapy helps couples, either married or unmarried to adjust with each other. It helps individuals to understand the dynamics of their relationship as well as how their personality is having an impact on the other person as well as their relationship. Therapies generally tend to focus on partner's interaction, and relationship. Relationship therapy generally deals with following issue:

- Infidelity
- Partner abuse
- Self-awareness

Therapists encounter certain problems which are unique to relationship therapy:

(a) Aggression and violence displayed by one partner towards the other partner.

(b) Rigidity and irrational approach adopted by one partner who is not ready to listen to what the therapist is saying.

(c) Advance hidden agenda of one of the partners.

The main job of the therapist, in relationship therapy, is three fold:

(a) Help clients become aware of how they treat each other.

(b) The subtle ways in which they, may hurt, insult, ignore others.

(c) How they may nurture each other.

3. Family Therapy: Family therapy involves the use of family members such as children, adolescents, and their parents to solve a particular problem. Family patterns and interaction among family members are important elements that need to be understood and corrected. There are many different types of family therapy. Family therapies are based on the assumption that families function as systems and hence individual's problems are best understood and treated as integral part of the family milieu (environment).

Many a times it so happens that a child who has been brought to a counselor or therapist may be the most vulnerable and sensitive person and that the real problem may lie with some other family member, say father or mother. In such a case family therapy may be of considerable use. Many a times the problem faced by an indivual may be some other problem such as marital discord, divided loyalty, expressing one's frustration and confusion, etc. In such cases helping the family members to understand family dynamics and changing the behaviour and perception plays an important role in helping them to adjust.

4. Biomedical Therapies: Biomedical therapies are strategies that rely on direct physiological intervention to treat the symptoms of psychological disorder. Since psychological disorders are result of biochemical abnormalities, they can be treated by biochemical therapies, which include use of psychoactive drugs. Some important categories of drugs and biomedical therapies are as follows:

(a) Anti-anxiety Drugs: These are drugs that are used primarily for alleviating anxiety, including minor tranquilizers. These are prescribed either by family physician or a psychiatrist. These drugs are generally used in the treatment of:

- Anxiety disorders.
- Stress-related disorders.
- Withdrawal from alcohol or other drugs.

The most common side effects of these drugs include:

- Fatigue
- Drowsiness
- Impaired Motor Co-ordination

These Drugs can be dangerous or fatal when used in combination with Alcohol or other Central Nervous System Depressants. These drugs are generally highly useful on a short term basis.

(b) Anti-depressant Drugs: These drugs are generally used to treat mood disorders. They help to increase the level of certain neurotransmitters especially Nor-epinephrine and Serotonin. These drugs generally help to relieve many of the typical symptoms of depression, such as:

- Sleeplessness or excessive sleepiness.
- Chronic fatigue.

- Loss of appetite.
- Loss of sex drive.
- Sadness.
- Feeling of worthlessness.

The greatest drawback of these medicines is that it takes 2-4 weeks for these drugs to take effect.

(c) Lithium: It is one type of drug used in the treatment of Mood Disorders. It is especially used to treat people with Bipolar Disorder. It can help to treat 75 per cent of manic episodes, as well as some cases of depression. One of the problems with this medicine is that the effective dose is close to toxic dose. Hence, it should be closely and carefully monitored.

(d) Anti-psychotic Drugs: This class of drugs is generally used to treat severe disorder such as Schizophrenia. It is used in the elevation of psychotic symptoms such as extreme agitation, hyperactivity, hallucinations and delusions. These classes of drugs are thought to work by blocking the activity of Dopamine and other neurotransmitters, thereby reducing hallucinations, delusions and bizarre behaviour. Two major drawbacks of these drugs are as follows:

- They do not cure apathy, social withdrawal or interpersonal difficulties found among Schizophrenia individuals.
- They have side effects. One such side effect is called as **Tardive Dyskinesia.** It is characterized by jerking movements around the neck and face and involuntary protrusions of the tongue.

(e) Electro-convulsive Therapy (ECT): ECT involves the administration of an electric current to the patient's brain to produce a convulsion. The patient is given a current of anywhere between 70 to 130 volts for a fraction of second, causing convulsions for a minute or so. The most common side effects of ECT is memory loss, especially the recall of events before treatment.

(f) Psychosurgery: It involves destroying or disconnecting brain tissues in an attempt to regulate abnormal behavior. It is also called as prefrontal lobotomy.

5. Community-based Service: It is a general term meaning that mental health services are located in the individual's own community or nearby. These services include:

(a) Day Hospitals: These hospitals provide part-time care in hospital setting for those with mental disorders. In these centers treatment is provided to patients from morning to evening and they are allowed to return to their families or home.

(b) Halfway Houses: It consists of a residential accommodation/ place in which the newly released patients and ex-addicts can live under supervision for a short period of time. Halfway Houses are also called group homes and board-and-care homes.

Halfway houses are small residences that are staffed by para-professionals who help the residents learn to live together and acquire the appropriate skills for returning to community life.

(c) Crisis Intervention: Individuals who face certain crises may occasionally require treatment for a short period. Such a treatment is called as Short Term Crises Counseling. Crises Intervention can range from one to five sessions. One type of Crises Intervention is ***Telephone Hotlines***.

Community-based Services are often found to be deficient with regards to finance, facilities and manpower.

How Well Does Therapy Work?

One of the most important debatable issues with respect to psychotherapy is that does it work? Which therapy is better? Three major questions about the effectiveness of therapy that has been investigated include:-

(i) Is therapy better than no therapy?
(ii) Is one particular type of therapy more effective than others?
(iii) Are certain disorders more amenable to certain therapies?

We would discuss each of these in brief:

(i) Is therapy better than no therapy? Long ago, Hans Eysenck (1966) concluded that overt time "clients not in therapy improved as much as did clients in therapy". In other words, extensive studies over last few decades have confirmed that therapy tends to have positive effects. The Commission appointed by American Psychiatric Association on Psychotherapy (2004) found that the average treated person is 80 % better than untreated patient. Similarly, in 1998 American Psychological Association concluded that "there is convincing evidence that people who have undergone several sessions of psychotherapy were found to be better than untreated individuals with respect to their emotional difficulties.

It was found that 50 per cent of patients noticeably improved after 08 sessions, while 75 % of individuals in Psychotherapy improved by the end of six months.

Factors influencing Psychotherapy: With respect to question as to what factors influence the effectiveness of psychotherapy the following points are worth nothing:

(a) Match between the client and therapists: The client and therapist must match in their personality and temperament for therapy to be effective. Individuals having certain types of personality are better clients for therapy. For e.g., Psychoanalyisis has been found to be more effective with clients who are ruminative, self-reflective and introspective.

(b) Becoming an active consumer of information: Individuals who are active consumer of information are likely to do better as compared to those who don't seek any information.

(c) Length of Treatment: It has been observed that longer treatments yield better results. One study (Donohue *et.al.*, 2000) found that those who had undergone 20 or more sessions did better as compared to those who had fewer sessions.

(d) Other factors: Some other factors that makes psychotherapy effective are as follows:

- focusing on skill building.
- aiding problem solving.
- repeated assessment.

(e) Therapist Characteristics: Some important characteristics of therapists that increase the effectiveness of therapy are as follows:

1. flexibility
2. honesty
3. respect for the client
4. trustworthiness
5. warmth
6. openness
7. unconditional positive regard, etc.

(f) Therapeutic Techniques: Some important therapeutic techniques that increases the effectiveness of therapy arc as follows:

- reflection.
- accurate interpretation.
- facilitation of expression of affect.
- free exploration of ideas and emotions.

(ii) Is one particular type of therapy more effective than others? This is the second most important question with respect to how well does therapy work? Research studies have shown that there is little difference among different types of interpersonal psychotherapy and that all are equally effective.

(iii) Are certain disorders more amenable to certain therapies: Do certain therapies work better with certain types of disorders? Research studies have revealed that certain types of therapies are better for certain disorders. For example:

(a) Cognitive behavior therapies appear to be effective for anxiety disorders and depression.

(b) Psychoactive drugs are more affective for treating schizophrenic disorders.

Some important points with respect to effectiveness of therapy are also worth noting:

1. Therapy is not exclusively dependent upon therapist's skills, the disorder and the type of therapy.
2. Client's traits and motives influence the effectiveness of therapy.

The following individuals are likely to benefit the most from psychotherapy:

1. Those who are articulate.
2. Those who are highly motivated.
3. One who are anxious to change.
4. Those capable of becoming personally involved in therapy.

Cultural, ethnic and educational factors also influence the effectiveness of therapy. For example Asian and Hispanic Americans tend to underutilize mental health care services, ethnic minorities drop out of therapy, etc.

Questions

1. Define Psychotherapy and discuss the Goals of Therapy.
2. Discuss the different types of Insight Therapies.
3. Discuss the different types of Cognitive-behavioural Therapies.
4. Write Short Notes on the following:
   (a) Group Therapies.
   (b) Relationship Therapy.
   (c) Family Therapy.
   (d) Biomedical Therapies.
   (e) Community-based Services.
5. Discuss the different issues with respect to Effectiveness of Therapy.

****

10 Good Grief and Death

Death of loved one or those who are close to us is an emotionally disturbing experience. Most of us fear death or avoid discussing about it. Psychologist have studied the phenomenon of death and human response to it. Many issues related to death, dying and grief has been topics of research interest.

DEATH AND DYING

Death is generally defined as cessation of life as measured by the absence of breathing, heartbeat and electrical activity of the brain. Many individuals, with respect to death, indulge in "denial" behavior. These individuals avoid talking about death, keep away from funerals, etc.

Denial about death means avoiding discussing about death. Denial helps to keep our anxiety level over the threat of our own demise at a low, manageable level. Denial also helps us to avoid thoughts of being separated from loved ones, whose relationship to us is essential to our self-esteem and well-being. Many individuals also consider it futile to think about death because they are not certain as to what comes after death. Denial of death in spite of its advantages has many disadvantages.

- Denial of death, especially our own death can make us indulge in certain defensive behavior which can keep us away from reality of life.
- Denial of death makes us avoid the aged, seriously ill, who may remind us of our own mortality.

Risks of Dying: Many people avoid taking risks as they are high on death anxiety or worry about dying. Individuals are not realistic about estimating the risk of dying.

- People tend to over estimate the risk of death from sensational causes such as accidents and homicides.
- Individuals underestimate the risk of death from non-spectacular causes such as heart attacks, strokes and diabetes.
- People underestimate the risk of death from familiar hazards such as smoking, surgery and diseases.

Such misjudgments arise from our tendency to believe that an event is likely to occur if we can easily imagine or recall it. Media also highlights certain events. It over reports dramatic and negative events, such as accidents and homicides. Newspapers report news about death arising from accidents and homicides more dramatically as compared to deaths due to disease.

Risk of dying varies with regard to lifestyle, heredity and gender.

(a) Those who smoke or are over-weight die earlier as compared to those who do not smoke or are of normal weight.

(b) Personality and stress is also co-related with death. Individuals who are hostile and easily angered tend to die sooner than those who are relaxed and easy going.

(c) People with long-lived parents and grand-parents tend to live longer than those whose close relatives die before 50.

Awareness of Death: Many of us lack awareness about death. If you are asked "How often do you think about your own death?", most people answer it "occasionally". In fact, our personal awareness of death fluctuates somewhat everyday.

- Most of the time we have very little awareness of death. We avoid thinking about the possibility of our death.
- On certain occasions we are more aware that our life span is limited and that we would die, especially if we have witnessed the death of a close friend or relative.
- When individuals are questioned directly about death, they rarely admit being fearful of it. When questioned with more indirect methods, such as fantasy and imagery, people express greater fears of death.

Personal awareness of death also varies somewhat by age. Surprisingly, people in the late 20's are most fearful of death, perhaps they have most of their lives ahead. The recent terrorist attacks have made people, especially youths, more sensitive to awareness of death. Most youths experience death due to suicide, accidents, or homicides. This indicates that death comes to them cruelly and tragically.

Individuals also think about their death as they approach late adulthood. Such individuals generally think about death more often and talk about it more openly. It has been observed that old people are usually less fearful of death than other age groups.

Near-Death Experiences: It refers to the distinctive state of recall associated with being brought back to life from the verge of death. Individuals who encounter accidents or undergo some major critical surgery and have been in a state of unconsciousness and on life support systems and then become normal are said to have undergone Near-Death Experience. Such individuals with Near-Death Experience have the following experience.

- They have experienced detachment from their bodies, feeling that they have seen pulled through a dark tunnel.
- Such individuals also experience being in a "spiritual body" in which physical objects present no barrier and movements from one place to another. In this state they also experience a reunion with long-last friends and loved ones.
- In Near-Death Experience individuals also experience the appearance of a brilliant light perceived as warm and loving.
- Finally people report being drawn back through the dark tunnel and undergoing a rapid re-entry into their bodies.
- As a result of Near-Death Experience, there is profound change in attitudes. Individuals who have gone through Near-Death Experience not only become less fearful of death but are also more concerned with loving and valuing life.
- There is also an increase in spirituality as well as more concern for others and less concern for material possessions.

The Experience of Dying: The term "Experience of Dying" refers to sequence of physiological and psychological changes experienced by individuals who are dying. One of the best known experts who have studied terminally ill patients and those "about to die" is Elizabeth Kubler-Ross. According to her, there are many overlapping stages of dying, some of which are as follows:

(a) Denial of death.

(b) Resentment.

(c) Bargain for time.

(d) Depression.

(e) Acceptance.

We would discuss each of these stages briefly.

(a) Denial of Death: It is the first stage of dying in which individuals experience "denial". They react with characteristic feeling "No, not me, this cannot happen to me". According to Zimmerman (2004) such denial protects them from the deep emotions associated with death and provides time to cope with the disturbing facts.

(b) Resentment: During this stage, dying person experience resentment especially towards individuals who are healthy. They generally ask the following questions "why me?" They experience envy, jealousy, anger, etc., especially when they see others enjoying life. The dying often takes their feelings out on those who are close to them. Caretakers and others close to dying people who are targets of such resentment should not take remarks personally but help the dying individuals to express their feelings.

(c) Bargain for Time: Dying individuals often attempts to negotiate with god to help them live longer. They often say "God should help me to live few years longer only till my daughter gets married... or my son gets a job", etc. They often bargain for time from God, doctors, parents, etc.

(d) Depression: It refers to intense and sometimes unrealistic sadness. It is important that the dying person is allowed to grieve and express sadness. Individuals who are in the process of dying often experience and display depression.

(e) Acceptance: Large majority of the individuals undergoing death generally reach this stage during which they accept death and have disengaged themselves from others. Most people prefer to die at home, though most eventually die in the hospital.

According to Elizabeth Kubler-Ross the experience of dying is not a fixed, inevitable process and that many people do not follow these stages. For some, anger remains the dominant mood throughout, whereas others are depressed till the end. According to some experts, individual differences are more pronounced in the experience of dying than are differences in stages of growth and development.

BEREAVEMENT AND GRIEF

The term bereavement means "to be deprived of". It is the process of adjusting to the experience of loss, especially to the death of friends or loved ones. It involves the overall experience of loss. Grief refers to the intense emotional suffering that accompanies our experience of loss. Mourning refers to the outward expression of bereavement and grief.

Grief Work: It refers to the healthy process of working through the emotions associated with loss. Grief work consists of the following:

- Freeing ourselves emotionally from deceased.
- Readjusting to life without that person.
- Resuming ordinary activities and
- Forming new relationships.

Grief process parallels the experience of dying and involves many of the same emotions. Simply discussing our grief with others, however, may not alleviate the grief. Grief work takes time and is not always completed.

There are individual differences in how people grieve but the typical experience is as follows:

- Initially we react to a person's death with a sense of shock and disbelief, especially when death occurs unexpectedly.
- In the case of terminally ill persons our response is subdued and accompanied by a sense of relief.
- After the initial shock wears off we are likely to be bothered by memories of the deceased. During this stage negative emotions such as anger and guilt are likely to surface. We are likely to blame God, fate or those who have been taking care of the deceased.

A few people often blame the deceased person for abandoning them, especially if person has committed suicide.

We may also feel guilty because of something we said or did

or felt we should have done while the person was still alive. Some of our guilt may be "survivor's guilt" that is, feeling guilty simply because we are still alive and the other person is not.

Emotional intensity of grief is often experienced in a disguised manner in the form of physical symptoms especially among older adults. The common symptoms of grief are:

- Crying.
- Depressed feelings.
- Loss of appetite.
- Difficulty in concentrating at work or home.
- Lack of interaction with others.

During the final stage of grief we often come to terms with our loss and resume our everyday activities. This stage may occur anytime from a few months to a year or more after the initial loss, depending on how close we are to the person and the circumstances surrounding the death. Normally one year, is the norm for normal grief work. In many cases normal grief may extend beyond one year also.

After one year depression and other emotional reactions to the death of loved one generally decline. After a year we are likely to recall deceased person with pleasant memories.

Unresolved Grief: Unresolved grief is a psychological state in which a person's emotional reaction to loss remains repressed, often being manifested in unexplained psychological and physical symptoms. It is also called as a Complicated Grief. It is prolonged and impairing type of grief.

Psychological Reactions: Many psychological reactions are related to grief:

(a) One such type of reaction is *avoidance behaviour*. In this form of behaviour grieving individuals avoid visiting a hospital or entering a room where the dead person was during the last period of his/her life.

(b) A few people react to unresolved grief in a *disguised manner*. They may displace their resentment or express it in many subtle forms after a long period of time.

(c) Yet another psychological reaction to unresolved grief is rumination about the death. Rumination means excessive preoccupation about death and constantly thinking in detail about the dead person. This type of rumination is detrimental for one's well-being and requires intervention by a trained psychologist.

Physical Reactions: The physical reactions of unresolved grief includes, as follows:

- Proneness to certain illnesses such as heart disease, strokes, cirrhosis of liver, hypertension and cancer as well as premature death.
- Widowed men between the ages of 55 and 65 dies, at 60 per cent higher rate than married men of same age. The most likely explanation is that the quality of life changes more drastically for men than for women, possibly because of their greater reliance on wives for their emotional and daily needs.

Good Grief: Grief for many people is a learning experience. It helps them to grow. There are many positive aspects of grief.

(a) One important positive aspect of grief is that it helps to appreciate loved ones and friends more fully despite their shortcomings.

(b) Another positive aspect of grief is that it helps us to value our relations with those who are living.

A good grief means that we have learned and grown in our bereavement more effectively.

There are several ways to make the experience of bereavement more effective.

- Talking it out
- Feeling it out and
- Acting it out.

Talking it out: While talking to the bereaved, focus on their feelings. Allow them to talk and listen carefully to what they say. Do not offer advice and suggestion. Allow the person to talk to you and do not interrupt them.

Feeling it Out: Helping the bereaved person to express his/her feelings, lightens the burden, reduces depression and makes the person feel good.

Men usually have more difficulty expressing bereavement largely because our society still considers a show of emotion by men to be a sign of weakness. It should be remembered that the characteristic way of expressing emotion varies from individual to individual. Some cry openly, others may just weep or have moistened eyes. Some may express their emotions in a hysterical manner such as expressing and pounding the wall with their fists.

Acting It Out: Some individuals overcome grief by acting out. There are many different ways of expressing grief through acts.

- Some individuals walk briskly so as to alleviate the tension and sadness of bereavement, at least temporarily.
- Funeral rituals offer an outlet to grief.
- Some individuals take care of the affairs of the deceased. This is therapeutic and helpful for the bereaved. For e.g., after the death of a father, the son would be faced with numerous litigations and claims. He will have to respond to it. This may burden him, at times he would feel angry but when viewed positively it offers an individual an opportunity for doing something for the deceased so that his or her soul rests in peace and thereby one feels better in serving the dead. Doing the work of deceased is one way of showing love and respect towards the dead as well as helping them to express their grief.
- Individuals who are resilient or hardy are more likely to indulge in problem-focused coping than emotional-focused coping during bereavement.

Those individuals who have adequate social support are less likely to be depressed and may recover from their grief faster. Some scholars are of the view that grief therapy that helps the bereaved to cope with death of the loved one is effective in helping the survivors cope with intense grief.

LIFE AND DEATH IN PERSPECTIVE

Life expectancy has increased from 48 years in 1955 to 65 years in 1995 to 75 years at present. As life expectancy has increased, individuals have to learn to deal with chronic diseases such as many forms of cancers, heart disease, kidney failures, etc.

Having health insurance or better income help you to die with better care. Because individuals are living longer and dying from chronic rather than acute illness, death comes more slowly and occurs in hospitals. Some important issues related to life and death are as follow:

1. The Right to Die
2. Natural Death
3. Funeral and Other Services
4. Death and Growth.

We would discuss each of the above topics in detail.

1. Right to Die: This is one of the most debatable, controversial and ethical issue. Do terminally ill patient have a right to die? Can one decide to stop treatment and remove life supports resulting in one's death? The right to die is a legal and ethical view which holds that individuals have the right to die. It holds the view that competent individuals who understand treatment choices and their consequences have a right to decide their own fate, such as withholding treatment that would delay death. One of the ethical dilemmas is, should doctors continue to support and keep an individual alive or should he alleviate an individual's suffering. Should family members continue to support and keep a person alive in a vegetative state or should they stop treatment and hasten the death of their loved one. There are two views with regard to right to die:

(a) Terminally ill patients in great pain should be allowed to die.
(b) Physician-assisted suicide, in which the physician administers a drug to a patient that results in his or her death. Physician assisted suicide has become a highly controversial issue throughout the world.

In USA, President's Commission on this issue including doctors, lawyers, theologians and others have concluded that competent patients who are able to understand treatment choice and their consequences have an all but absolute right to decide their fate. When a person is incompetent, a surrogate, usually a family member, should be given the authority to decide. One important concept related to this is that of **"Living Will"** in which a person instructs doctors and family members to stop using life-sustaining procedures in the event of terminal condition. In USA, a new law has made provision for all federally funded hospitals, nursing homes and hospices to tell incoming patient of their right to write a living will. It is also sometimes called advanced directives or health care proxies. In some countries, right-to-die exists, which makes these directives binding on the doctors. Living Wills involves considerable controversy and issues that needs more debate. Because Living Wills and Health Care Proxies are relatively new to our society, time, experience and more research is required to sort out all of the advantages and dis-advantages of this new system of dying.

One of the greatest drawbacks of the right-to-die movement is that it can program an individual to die quickly and may come in the way of the desire to live in spite of all odds.

Organ Donation Card: It is a system which permits doctors and/or relatives of the patients who have died suddenly to offer the organs of the dead patient as donation to those who need it urgently. Organ donation requires immediate transplantation of vital organs from someone who has died to a living person in need of the organ.

2. Natural Death: Natural death means helping the people to die at their own pace and style. One important topic related to natural death is hospice.

Hospice: The hospice movement is aimed at achieving greater support and humane approach in dealing with people who are about to die soon. In middle Ages, hospice was a shelter for travellers who had nowhere else to go. Today, the term hospice refers to taking care of those about to die. Hospice is a system of care that integrates a physical facility for terminally ill with the patient's family and home to enable the patient to die with dignity. Some of the advantages of hospice are as follows:

- Helping in pain control.
- Preparing meals.
- Offering emotional support and guidance to family members.
- It is economical, offers humane treatment and provides social atmosphere for the dying patients.

Hospice stay should be of three months to have a desired effect.

3. Funerals and Other Services: The term funeral means ceremony and rituals associated with the burials or cremation of the dead.

In societies which have a strong belief in life-after death, funerals were held for the benefit of the dead. Death was viewed as a passage to heaven or eternal life. Some ancients not only buried the corpse but also buried their personal items with their body (corpse) to be used on the "journey" to eternal life.

Although it is the dead who are remembered at the funerals, the ceremony often is for the benefit of the survivors. Funerals have become expensive and the matter of status, where family members choose on the basis of status and emotions rather than commonsense.

According to one estimate funerals are typically the fourth-largest consumer purchase following house, car and wedding.

4. Death and Growth: Death is considered to be an integral part of life that gives meaning to human existence and, in fact, can foster further growth.

- Death sets limit to our life, reminding us to spend our days on the things that matter the most.
- Individuals who have recovered from intense mourning also learn to deal and cope with other adverse events of their lives.
- Grieving over the loss of loved one helps us to relate more deeply with those who are alive.

If an individual begins to view death as an inevitable companion of life, it may help you to live fully rather than passively.

It should be remembered that usually, it is those who have not lived their life fully who are most reluctant to die. Haunted by broken relationship and unfulfilled dreams, they grow even more anxious and fearful in the face of death.

Thinking about one's own death may give a new perspective in life. For example, if you were told that you had only a limited time to live, how would you spend time? What unfinished task would you be most concerned with? Which people would you most want to be with? Pondering the answers to such questions may help to clarify what is really important to you. Realistic awareness of death and dying can help to live our present life meaningfully.

Questions

1. Discuss the different issues related to Death and Dying?
2. Write short notes on the following:
   (a) Near-Death-Experience.
   (b) Stages of Dying.
3. Define Bereavement and Grieving and discuss the various issues related to it.
4. Write short note on the following:
   (a) Grief Work
   (b) Unresolved Grief
   (c) Good Grief
5. Discuss the various issues related to Death and Life in Perspective.
6. Write short note on the following:
   - The Right to Die
   - Natural Death
   - Funeral and Other Services
   - Death and Growth

****

PATTERN OF QUESTION PAPER

Pattern of Question Paper to be brought into force with effect from the academic year 2009-2010 at S.Y.B.A. Psychology - Revised syllabi

Paper II (Social Psychology), Paper III (Developmental Psychology), and General Applied Component (4 options - A - Health Psychology; B - Psychology of Adjustment; C - Stress Management; and D - Psychology of Gender)

Duration of examination = 2 hours; Marks = 50 (in each term)

1. Question No. 6 is compulsory; any three more questions to be attempted out of the remaining five questions.
2. The first 5 questions carry 12 marks each, and Question No. 6 carries 14 marks.
3. Q. No. 1, 2, 3, 4 and 5 will be on the 5 topics covered in the term. Any one Question of these can have 2 parts, A and B, each having 6 marks, or all 5 questions can be full length essay-type.
4. Question No. 6 – Write 4 short notes out of 5, each of 3 1/2 marks; one short note will be from each of the 5 topics.

Pattern of Question Paper for A.T.K.T. examination of 100 marks of Psychology Papers I, II, III and Applied Components to be brought into force with effect from the academic year 2009-2010 (Revised syllabi)

F.Y.B.A. Psychology Paper I, S.Y.B.A. Papers II and III (Social and Developmental Psychology), and General Applied Component (4 options - Health Psychology, Psychology of Adjustment, Stress Management, and Psychology of Gender)

Duration = 3 hours Marks = 100 (50 marks per section)

1. There will be 6 questions in each Section, 12 questions in all. Three questions from each Section are to be attempted, 6 questions in all.
2. Q. No. 1, 2, 3, 4, 5 and 6 in Section I will be on the 5 topics covered in the first term and Q. No. 7, 8, 9, 10, 11, and 12 in Section II will be on the 5 topics covered in the second

term.

3. Question Nos. 6 and 12 carry 18 marks and are **compulsory-** Write 3 short notes out of 5, each of 6 marks; one short note will be from each of the 5 topics covered in each term.
4. The remaining 10 questions carry 16 marks each. Any 2 questions are to be attempted out of these questions **from each Section.**
5. A-B type of questions may be asked, but not more than 1 out of the 5 questions in each Section.

Book for Study

Duffy, K.G., & Atwater, E. (2008). *Psychology for Living – Adjustment, Growth, and Behaviour Today.* (9th ed.). New Jersey: Pearson Prentice Hall

Books for reference

1. Bam, B. P. (2008). *Winning Habits: Techniques for Excellence in Sports.* New Delhi: Pearson Power, Dorling Kindersley India Pvt. Ltd.
2. Baumgardner, S., & Crothers, M. (2009). *Positive Psychology.* Pearson Education.
3. Brannon, L., & Feist J. (2007). *Introduction to Health Psychology.* Thomson Wadworth. New Delhi: Indian edition.
4. Greenberg, J. S. (2008). *Comprehensive Stress Management.* (10th ed). McGraw-Hill Publications.
5. Hariharan, M., & Rath, R. (2008). *Coping with Life Stress: The Indian Experience.* New Delhi: Sage Publications India Pvt. Ltd.
6. Schafer, W. (2002). *Stress Management.* (4th ed). New Delhi: Wadsworth Cengage Learning India Pvt. Ltd., First Indian reprint 2008.
7. Snyder, C.R., & Lopez, S.J. (2007). *Positive Psychology – The scientific and practical explorations of human strengths.* New Delhi: Sage Publications India Pvt. Ltd., South Asia edition.
8. Taylor S. E. (2003). *Health Psychology* (5th Ed). McGraw-Hill Higher Education. International Edition.
9. Weiten, W., & Lloyd, M.A. (2006). *Psychology Applied to Modern Life - Adjustment in the 21st Century.* (8th ed.) Cengage Learning India.
10. Wilson, E. (2007). *Stress Proof Your Life: 52 Brilliant Ideas for Taking Control.* New Delhi: Pearson Power.

****